MINI ENCYCLOPEDIA OF
DOG TRAINING
& BEHAVIOR

MINI ENCYCLOPEDIA OF
DOG TRAINING
& BEHAVIOR

*Learn from an expert how to obedience train
your dog and remedy behavioral problems
and bad habits*

Colin Tennant

BARRON'S

First edition for the United States and Canada
Published in 2006 by Barron's Educational Series, Inc.

First published in 2006 by Interpet Publishing
© Copyright 2006 by Interpet Publishing

All inquiries should be addressed to:
Barron's Educational Series, Inc.
250 Wireless Boulevard
Hauppauge, NY 11788
http://www.barronseduc.com

ISBN-13: 978-0-7641-3238-4
ISBN-10: 0-7641-3238-5

Library of Congress Catalog Card Number 2004117787

Printed and bound in China
19 18 17 16 15 14 13

This book sets out to explain how to train a dog in a 21-day program. It gives advice on various training exercises and certain measures that can be used to remedy bad behavior. When used sensibly, the programs described in this book are quite safe, but readers must be aware that some dogs are powerful animals that may, on occasion, behave unpredictably. Dogs that display characteristics such as aggression should always be approached with caution; if in doubt, seek the advice of a qualified dog trainer or behavior practitioner first.

The information and recommendations in this book are given without any guarantees on behalf of the author and publisher, who disclaim any liability with the use of this material.

The Author

Colin Tennant is Britain's leading expert in dog behavior and obedience training. He operates a canine behavior center providing advice and assistance for owners of dogs of all breeds. In 1975 he served in the Cheshire Police Dog Section and is Home Office—qualified as a police dog handler. Colin began his career in canine behavior and obedience training at the Asoka Training School in Manchester. In the early 1980s he founded the London Dog Training Group specializing in one-to-one training for problem dogs.

Colin has trained animals for more than 100 television programs and has made several instructional videos dealing with training problems as well as the care of cats and other pets. He lectures around the world and is a frequent contributor to national newspapers and magazines. He is employed as a consultant by the media. Colin has provided expert advice on dog behavior and training to the BBC and other national TV networks, as well as to radio programs and filmmakers. He is chairman of the Canine and Feline Behavior Association based in Great Britain and senior pet behavior practitioner working at his Canine and Feline Behaviour Centre situated in Hertfordshire. He is the author of *Breaking Bad Habits In Dogs* and *21 Days To Train Your Dog*.

How To Navigate Your Way Around This Book

The purpose of this book is to show readers how they can train a dog to an acceptable level of obedience in just three weeks. The basic disciplines covered are walking to heel, the sit, stand and down positions, and the associated stays that can be used with them, and the recall. Various methods of training these disciplines are featured so that if one tactic is not successful with a particular dog, readers will have a number of alternatives with which to experiment instead. The timetable for the training program is outlined on pages 72–75 while the exercises themselves occupy pages 76–199.

Before that, a number of introductory chapters are included (pages 8–37) that introduce readers to dog psychology, the thinking that underlies the training methods recommended, the necessary equipment that will be needed, simple ways of training a puppy, and the most effective methods of communicating commands to a dog. Importantly, a chapter entitled The Leadership Program (pages 20–27) also explains how owners can use a knowledge of dog psychology to establish their position as leader of the family pack. This understanding helps to define many aspects of a relationship with a dog and enhances a trainer's ability to command obedience.

The central section of the book (pages 38–71) addresses common problem behaviors that some dogs exhibit in the domestic environment. It examines why they arise and offers a number of simple, well-proven solutions to help owners overcome these bad habits. It is hoped that this combination of information about behavior and training will help dog owners to enjoy better one of the great pleasures open to us—a harmonious and loving relationship with a well-adjusted and well-behaved dog.

Contents

1 • What Is Training?

Dog training means different things to different owners. For some it's a case of simply waiting for the right time and then joining a local club with their puppy and completing a course lasting about eight weeks. Other people consider the matter solved by training their puppy or adult dog themselves. This is especially true of dog owners who have had dogs before—in other words, experienced dog owners. Training dogs is open to all sorts of interpretation, and the different techniques that can be used often confuse the person about to embark on training a dog. Added to this, the dog has its own drives that don't include walking endlessly in circles in a club. Dogs require motivational work to maintain their interest—just like people.

I have trained many thousands of dogs from a very early age. My experience has taught me a good deal about dog psychology, training methods, and owners and their expectations—what they want and how they understand the

Right: *Dogs that jump up at people are pests—they need proper training.*

dog. The knowledge I have acquired will be critical in giving you the best practical advice as you begin to train your dog. It is pragmatic and based soundly on experience.

The Behavioral Aspect of Training

Some people whose dogs cause them anguish own dogs with aggression problems. This may involve aggression toward people, toward other canines, or both. Many of the situations are complex. Though these dogs exhibit aggression, if the dog is trained to a high standard of obedience, a powerful element of control is introduced into the equation that can effectively stem, or at least control, the aggressive dog. It will not persuade the dog to like all the dogs or people it meets, but obedience stops the dog from attacking by the simple fact that it will come, sit, go

Left: *We can use training methods to interrupt a dog that is starting to show signs of aggression or antisocial behavior.*

down and stay when situations arise that cause friction.

Dogs that have phobias, anxieties, chase joggers, or are just simply too boisterous can also be assisted and controlled by dog training. An anxious dog is more likely to take a cue from a strong leader (you, the trainer). Your calmness and natural authority concentrate the dog's mind on you and what you are asking it to do rather than on the cause of its anxiety. Of course these types of dogs still require behavior programs to calm their anxieties or to redirect unwelcome chase behavior. However, a well-trained dog is easier to manage all round.

Above: *A well-trained dog that knows its place in the family hierarchy and integrates readily with people and other pets is a pleasure to own.*

The Well-Mannered Dog

Like a well-behaved child, obedience-trained dogs are certainly more welcome in most areas of our society. Although millions of us adore dogs, many people don't. So it is important for dog owners to give their dogs the best training possible. Unfortunately, human nature being what it is, in my experience too few people look at prevention by training dogs. Most people purchase books or videos when a problem is already developing. It's a bit like waiting for a car to break down before getting it serviced. Of course a dog, unlike the car, is a free-thinking, intelligent animal. Although my car may break down through my lack of care, a dog will exert its own will to pursue a course of action if we do not teach it what we want it to do. That is why this book concentrates principally on solutions and includes numerous training methods to help you to train your dog successfully.

The Challenges Awaiting You

You will be faced with a number of challenges, the first being to unravel the claims of so many experts regarding the best way to train a dog. Well, I hope to dispel any confusion and give clear advice on how to train your dog in a straightforward 21-day course that is described in detail in the second half of this book. Continual practice will cement the training and help your dog to become a well-adjusted pet. The old adage that practice makes perfect applies to dog training as to other skills in life. Dog training is not complicated or mysterious; it just involves learning another set of rules coupled with a wish to make proper contact with your dog—to form a bond through a new language that we call "dog training."

Training Techniques

Over the years, dog training techniques have improved and a more dog-friendly training philosophy has evolved that benefits both dogs and owners. We manipulate the dog's instincts and redirect those instincts into an activity that helps us train our dogs. For example, consider the dog's predatory behavior of chasing and catching prey. By substituting a ball for the prey and teaching the dog to pursue, catch, and bring back the ball, the dog's instinctive love of the chase is partly satisfied. With repetition we can use the ball as an object that the dog craves. The ball is then used as a reward to teach a dog to sit, stand, lie down, and stay, and it even helps with the recall exercise. It works in some, but not all,

1 *Many dogs have an instinctive love of pursuit that we can turn to our advantage in training.*

2 *Playing chase and retrieve games with a ball or toy taps into the dog's innate desire to hunt prey.*

cases—that is why this book offers tried-and-true methods in abundance. If one does not work, you have an alternative to try.

What Is a Trained Dog?

This question is open to much debate. My clients, who see me at the Canine and Feline Behaviour Centre, have as many ideas about what constitutes a trained dog as the variety of breeds they bring me to see. The most common statement I hear is that the dog is trained but it just won't come back when there are distractions in the park, such as other dogs, squirrels, or fascinating scents. So is the dog trained? The dogs certainly know what **"Come"** means as they amply demonstrate in the consulting rooms. I term this a convenient dog-training response. In other words, if the dog has nothing more interesting to do or if it has had its fun and is now a little tired, it responds. That is not a trained dog to my way of thinking.

Very few people need a dog to come to them unless there is a good reason to command it to do so—perhaps the animal is bothering other dogs or park users or is running off toward a dangerous, busy road. Dogs that come only of their own volition, not when they are commanded regardless of what is on their mind, are not obedience-trained dogs.

So the true definition of a trained dog is a dog that obeys you in all situations at your volition and command.

3 *By repeating the game many times over, the dog comes to value the toy as it now associates the toy with the excitement of the chase and the pleasure that it feels when praised for bringing the toy back.*

4 *The favorite toy can now become a valuable training aid, being used as a treat to reward the dog for performing exercises like the sit, stand, or heel correctly.*

Do We Need To Train Dogs?

To many readers, the answer seems an obvious "yes." However, many people, too many, either can't be bothered or don't see dog training as important. Dogs, of course, vary immensely. Different breeds have their own instinctive behavior. Because of this innate variability, some dog owners do little in the way of training and yet have few problems, in the same way as some parents have an easy time when rearing an individual child. Just because your dog naturally behaves well is not necessarily a reflection of your skill.

Training relies on clear communication. Verbal commands and hand signals help to make your meaning explicit.

The dog has very strong drives that can cause conflict. For instance, over a period of years one client of mine has had different generations of the same breed of dog from the same breeder and the offspring of similar breeding lines. He used more or less the same approach to training each generation and yet had three different results. Chance obviously plays its part. So if you have tried hard but your dog remains difficult, don't look upon yourself as a failure. I will endeavor in this book to help you become a leader first, a trainer second, and thirdly a dog owner who enjoys a close relationship with your dog.

By following the Leadership Program outlined in a subsequent chapter and psychologically taking charge and teaching your dog a very black-and-white style of obedience using a language that it understands and you can practice, a new, positive relationship can develop that is fair to the dog and you. The Leadership Program is critical psychological training that should take place before the mechanics of obedience training begins.

You will feel a real sense of achievement when your dog sits as obediently as this one when you start to put the sit/stay training into practice.

Above: *To become an effective trainer, you first have to become an effective leader. Your dog must look up to you as number one.*

Dogs and Children

When educated properly and using the ideas explained in this book, dogs can—and do—behave well socially with children. However, the idea that all dogs love children is just a myth. Many dogs don't like children, and especially small toddlers, especially if the dog is already established in the home and the children are later arrivals. Their animated, unpredictable behavior will sometimes spook a dog. So it is imperative that you select the right sort of dog and breed for your children's age group. Training your dog to be obedient has a big effect on control of the dog, but it is equally vital to control your children around dogs.

Once the child understands some of the elementary dos and don'ts of owning a dog, then even quite young children can be allowed to take part in aspects of dog training. It's best to train your dog to a reasonable level first and then slowly allow your children to practice some of the training commands—just a few at a time. Children's delivery of commands can be a hit-and-miss affair at first (especially with regard to consistency.) However, older children soon catch on, and then they too can enjoy training the dog and building up basic control skills. Children over the age of about ten can be allowed to walk dogs, but the safety rule I always bear in mind is if the dog panics or needs restraint, could the child hold the dog physically? So consider the size of your dog in relationship to the child before deciding whether the child can walk it, however trained it may be. Safety first.

2 • Training Equipment

Dog-training equipment is relatively inexpensive to buy considering how much you can achieve with it when it is used knowledgeably. Here's the most basic list of equipment that you will need for training your dog.

• A 4-foot (1.2 m) lead and also a 6-foot (2 m) one if you can run to it (leather is best).

• A collar, either fixed (meaning that it cannot tighten fully) or a half-check collar.

• A long line about 30–50 feet (10–15 m) in length made of thin strong nylon, with a dog hook attached to one end and a handling loop at the other. The long line is primarily used for the recall exercise (see pages 178–185). The line can be abrasive on the hands, so it pays to wear heavy gloves when using a long line for recall training.

• A short line about 6 feet (2 m) in length.

• A flexible lead—this is especially useful when training puppies.

Left: *The basic equipment required for dog training need not cost you a fortune. The absolute essentials are a good-quality collar and lead and a short and long line.*

As well as these basics, many other items are available that can prove useful. I shall outline these options in more detail below.

Body Harnesses

Dog body harnesses are useful when traveling with your dog in a car. They are similar to a child harness. Always place your dog on the rear seat if possible and fix the harness straps onto the seat belt for safety. Dogs that ride in a car this way are less likely to misbehave, and when car doors are opened, the dog cannot leap out.

Below and right: *Walking harnesses exert pressure under the front legs of dogs that pull.*

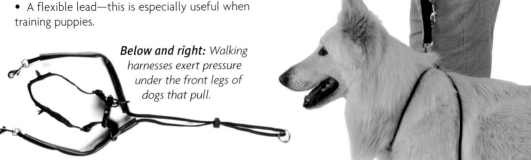

Above: *A body harness restrains the movement of a dog when it is traveling with you in the car.*

Walking Harnesses To Prevent Pulling

These harnesses are specifically designed to make pulling on the lead uncomfortable for a dog. They work by causing uncomfortable pressure under the dog's "armpits" under its front legs when it surges ahead—conversely, if the dog stops pulling there is no pressure on the sensitive skin surface under its legs. They work effectively on many dogs and don't require too much skill on the handler's part.

Flexible Lead Training (puppy safe)

A flexible lead (flexi) has many uses in training a dog. It is a long lead that extends and rewinds into a small plastic container that you hold by means of a handle. It has a button near the handle that

locks the line at any chosen position. Pressing the button again releases the line, which winds up onto a spool against the pressure of a spring. It's a good control device to use when walking young puppies when they are first being trained, and it keeps them safely under your control up to a distance of about 40 feet (12 m) depending on the model used.

Face Collars (head halters)

They help stop dogs pulling. Of all the heelwork aids, other than heelwork training itself, they are the most effective. At first they are often actively rejected by the dog and this can cause upset to the owner. The next page explains the best way of introducing a dog to wearing a face collar. The device fits over the dog's muzzle and head. It allows the dog's mouth to open as usual so the dog can breathe properly. When the dog pulls ahead of the owner, the head collar redirects the dog's head back to the owner's side, thereby making pulling uncomfortable and awkward for the dog. It teaches the dog that walking alongside you on a loose lead is the most comfortable option.

Left: *A flexi lead helps you to keep control of a dog when the time comes to introduce it to other pets in the home.*

15

Introducing The Face Collar

First get the dog to sit while wearing a lead and collar. Then have several juicy tidbits (such as cheese or ham) at hand. Put on the face collar (the dog must be able to open its mouth with the muzzle fitted), and then reward the dog with a tidbit through the gaps in the face collar. Leave it on the dog for a few minutes, then remove it, and give another food reward. The dog should now associate having the collar fitted with receiving a reward.

This needs to be repeated three times daily for about ten minutes' duration and

Right: *Face collars are very effective in helping to control dogs that pull persistently on the lead.*

for a further three days. On day four attach the lead and fit the head collar to the dog. Then walk the dog a few feet in the house or yard while rewarding the dog at short intervals. If the dog

panics or attempts to rub its head on the floor (which is normal), distract it with the food and use your lead to make it sit.

It's also useful to leave the muzzle on the dog in the house twice daily for about ten to fifteen minutes. When the dog begins to accept the muzzle without endless fuss, then you are beginning to reach normalization.

Most dogs resent the face collar at first but quickly adapt to it and associate it with food reward and walks. Once you can walk the dog around the house or yard without adverse reaction, you are ready for normal outdoor use.

The Food Toy and Other Playthings (puppy safe)

Certain well-made toys can be used in training. I use a toy called the Kong which is a type of hollow rubber chewy receptacle in which food can be concealed. The dog enjoys chewing away at the toy and picking out the morsels of food. It provides a pleasurable distraction on which the dog is happy to concentrate. It allows me to reward the dog for being attached to a hook and lead when I use this type of restraint in the Leadership Program. It immediately helps the dog to associate being tethered with a long-lasting reward as the dog tries to extract the food from the toy.

There are some good-quality, strong toys on the market. I generally use a solid rubber ball for retrieve. Tennis balls are unsafe because they can be

Right: *Dogs can spend ages happily gnawing away at a rubber food toy.*

The dog or puppy takes its unrewarding cue from its action of chewing, not from your previous action of spraying.

Below: *Bitter-smelling sprays can deter dogs that habitually chew their leads and other domestic objects.*

squashed in the dog's jaws only to resume their shape in its windpipe, causing serious harm. Rubber rings, rope toys, raggers, and other such toys all allow you to interact playfully with a dog, helping to develop its mind and its sense of enjoyment of being with you.

Deterrent Sprays (puppy safe)

Bitter apple or citronella are harmless, unpleasant-smelling liquids that can be sprayed onto objects. They can help to stop a dog from chewing the lead or grabbing it as part of a game. The spray is particularly effective at dissuading puppies from using the lead as another toy chew, which is natural puppy behavior.

Left: *Colorful and durable, dog toys come in many shapes and sizes.*

> **WARNING**
> **Chain Collars (check chains)**
> Check chains and slip collars tighten on a dog's neck when it pulls on the lead. They should be used only in very specific circumstances and under the guidance of a qualified trainer. They are not for general use and do **not** feature as training aids in this book.

Training Disks (puppy safe)

This training tool consists of five small metallic disks on a ring that clatter together noisily when they are thrown on the floor. Alternatively, you can throw a dog chain or an old bunch of blunt keys to make a similar noise. Sound deterrents like this are useful in stopping dogs in their tracks that are about to misbehave or

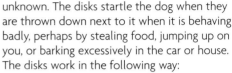

Training disks clatter when they hit the ground.

are already misbehaving. I use the command **"No"** in conjunction with the disks.

The psychology of sound training is that the dog does not understand where the sound is coming from and dogs are very suspicious of the unknown. The disks startle the dog when they are thrown down next to it when it is behaving badly, perhaps by stealing food, jumping up on you, or barking excessively in the car or house. The disks work in the following way:

• The dog learns a sound and unpleasant association (with whatever it is doing).

• It associates the sound with a command **"No."**

• Eventually it will respond instantly to the command **"No"** without the disks being used.

One word of caution: use disks with care with puppies and only if other methods have been tried and exhausted first.

Whistles (puppy safe)

A good-quality whistle is an essential when it comes to some of the methods of recall training that are described later in the book. A whistle carries further than the human voice so it is useful when you have to attract the attention of a dog that has wandered off out of earshot.

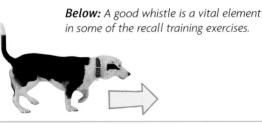

Below: A good whistle is a vital element in some of the recall training exercises.

Above: Small chunks of ham, cheese, and cooked chicken make very tasty food rewards.

Food Rewards (puppy safe)

I use only food rewards or tidbits in training. I do not give my dogs any food treats at any other time, so the dog does not learn that harassing people can produce food tidbits. I recommend ham, cheese, and chicken cut into very small chunks. This is natural, fresh, and far more appealing to dogs than manufactured, processed tidbits. They are easy to use and can be carried as appropriate in a plastic container or bag tucked into a pouch, fanny pack, or your pocket. Use treats sparingly.

A Good Diet (puppy safe)

Though food (as opposed to treats) is not a substance that is often referred to in training manuals, it can be a very potent influence over the way an animal behaves. Food is the vital ingredient of body maintenance, and it affects behavior in dogs. Most dog foods, canned or dried, contain chemicals and additives that are apparently safe, although this is a contentious issue, as it is with foods designed for human consumption. I personally believe that dogs should be fed a natural diet that is guaranteed free of chemicals or additives. This removes the chance that any colorings or other chemicals present in the diet may affect behavior. I call this a "clean diet."

I have found a considerable change in dogs' behavior when they are fed a clean diet of fresh meat cooked with vegetables and rice. Many hyperactive dogs change completely when their diet is changed to meat, two vegetables, and rice. Remember that training a dog is time-consuming, but training a dog that is detrimentally affected is much, much more difficult—so please consider diet carefully. A calm dog is an easier dog to train. You can test your dog by feeding it a natural-food diet for a month and observing the results yourself.

Left: Diet can affect a dog's behavior detrimentally, so it pays to choose what you feed your pet with care.

3 • *The Leadership Program*

The wolf's nature and patterns of behavior are present in your dog (irrelevant of breed), however altered its behavior may seem through domestication. The rules that govern the hierarchical order and smooth functioning of the wolf pack are the rules that your dog understands. It is the dominant or deferential positions by which wolves communicate that we are going to use to help you train your dog. We shall be using canine psychology, as well as repetitive dog training exercises, to achieve our goals. By manipulating the dog's natural drives, we can psychologically demote our dog, or at least teach it that it has to respect you as the leader and the rest of your family as higher-ranking members of your family pack.

Your dog may apparently be quite deferential already, but most dogs have learned how to manipulate people to suit their own ends. More often than not, we are unaware of our dog's determination to control situations in a daily routine. This can be something as simple as barging through doors first or seemingly as innocuous as demanding attention. These dominant/demanding behaviors by themselves may appear harmless. When combined with other behaviors, they can build up the dog's rank within your family pack. We call this dominant behavior, a term that does not mean aggressive.

The golden rule is you lead or are led. Now is the time to assert yourself and treat the dog in such a way that it will find a comfortable place at the bottom of the family pack.

Above: Deep down, a pet dog is a wolf in Labrador's (or any other breed's) clothing.

Right: Leadership puts you and your family at the top of the pack hierarchy.

How Does This Affect Training?

A dog that does not see you as a leader tends not to listen unless doing so suits its own purpose. Dogs that don't listen are more difficult to train and can get themselves into all sorts of conflict with us and the wider world around us. Even if your dog does not appear to be high ranking, the Leadership

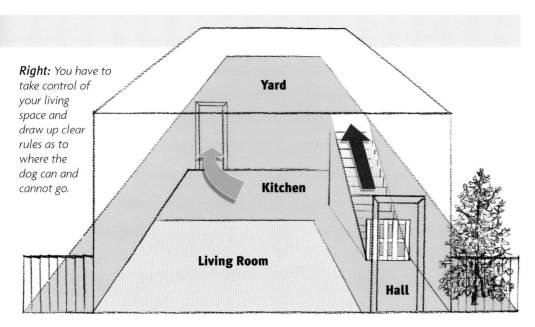

Right: *You have to take control of your living space and draw up clear rules as to where the dog can and cannot go.*

Yard

Kitchen

Living Room

Hall

Program will still help define many aspects of your relationship and enhance your ability to command obedience. It reduces any ambiguity in the relationship between you and your dog.

The essence of the program is that we remove a good deal of the time and affection we devote to our dogs when they are demanding it but give back that praise, touch, attention, and affection when it is linked to an action that the dog learns we want it to perform. We call this training. We are simply redistributing our kindness and attention, not totally denying the dog those rewards. We also block or ignore any action that the dog uses to get us to defer to it or any behavior that gives the dog an elevated view of its position within the family pack.

The House Plan

First off, let's look at the home front. We spend most of our time in the home with our dogs. Some of you will already have demarcated areas where the dog can and cannot go— others will have no such rules and allow the dog to use the house or apartment at will. I must clearly state that if you want to train your dog well, you will need to treat it like a dog and make sure that you call the shots in your own home. Moreover, once the dog understands the new rules, it will become calmer and more obedient as you develop your leadership role.

N.B. It is better to introduce the following program over a one- or two-week period before beginning the actual training course.

The House Plan

The Bedroom

The bedroom is attractive to many dogs because they can spend long periods of time there next to the leader, thereby giving them a very important privilege and, by extension, high rank. Your scent is powerful in this room and you—the leader—sleep here. Some people place a basket in the bedroom. From the dog's point of view, the room is the important element. It's not just the bed, it's the location and your presence there. So if your dog sleeps in your bedroom, ban it from now on. This helps to demonstrate to your dog that you are

Below: *Under the new regime, dogs no longer sleep in your bedroom.*

Even the stairs and landing become a "no-go" area.

unequivocally the leader. I also stop the dog from sleeping on landings or stairways. Using a baby gate erected in a suitable place helps you to enforce this rule.

The Living Room

If your dog has access to the living room or the main room in which you live, I want you to restrict this from now on. By excluding the dog for most of the time that you are relaxing, the dog again has its lower rank emphasized. Do allow the dog in periodically at your command. Perhaps play a game of ball and at the end of the game put the ball in a secure box and let the dog see you doing so. Then relax and only call it to you for a pat when you choose to do so. Of course that pat or stroke is not for free— it is a reward for coming on command. Then tell it to sit or lie down for a time and praise it accordingly. Please, no long, excited pats and strokes. Keep everything calm. After about half an hour or so, the dog must leave the room when told to for its usual place in the kitchen, hallway, or yard.

Easy Chairs

Dominant dogs, like their counterparts in the wild, like to occupy elevated positions and especially positions that we habitually take as our own. In a house that means the couch, comfortable chairs in the living room, and even, in the case of smaller dogs, your lap. My response to this is a big **"No."** Dogs that are given these privileges, and even a chair for themselves, feel entitled to assume the appropriate status. This again removes the line of demarcation between the leader and the led. So ban the dog from these places, and teach it to get off the furniture.

Move Out Of My Way

When walking about the house, make your dog get out of your way if it is blocking your path. When a leader walks tall, the other pack members make way. If the dog will not move by command, then slowly shuffle your feet toward it and as they touch the dog, it should move. Don't say **"Good boy"**—just walk on by. For obstinate dogs I often gently push a disconnected vacuum cleaner or floor brush ahead of me as I go so the dog gets the message. "Make way for the leader" is the order of the day.

Doorways And Gates

Many dogs like to push their way ahead of us through doorways or when a gate is opened. Why? Well, the leader leads. Even in human society, people of rank go first. In dog society, it is the leader should always go first. If your dog tries to surge ahead, simply slam the door shut quickly so it cannot go ahead of you. Open the door slightly, ease your body through first, and then call the dog on command. If it tries to push through in an undisciplined way, close the door again. Of course, you must make sure that the door does not hit the dog, but the noise of the door banging shut should bring the dog up short. Repeat as many times as necessary. If your dog is particularly large and/or determined, use a collar and lead for added control.

1-3 *Don't step around a dog that will not get out of your way. "Walk tall" and command the dog to* **"Move"**. *If that doesn't work, shuffle forwards with both feet. The dog will move when it feels the touch of your feet. Don't stop to praise it, just walk on by.*

No Free Rewards

Food, Treats, and Toys

• Try and feed your dog after you have enjoyed your main meal of the day. Wait about 30 minutes after you have eaten, and then feed your dog.

• Teach your dog to sit and wait to eat; it should only be allowed to start on your say so. I simply use the command **"Yours"** or **"Eat."**

• Don't allow the dog to beg and scrounge food from the table. Better still, don't allow it near your eating area.

• Because we use food a good deal in training, don't offer the dog any treats except when advised to do so during the training programs.

• Remove all the dog's toys for the immediate future, especially if you are going to use them as motivators during training. A toy is not such a delight for a dog in training if it can play with the same toy at any time it chooses. Discover the toy that your dog likes most and use that in training. Lock the rest away.

Petting and Stroking

This is undoubtedly the most difficult area on which to advise dog owners. I want you to stop petting your dog for free, or, as often is the case, when your dog demands it. I realize that there is little point in having a dog if you can't pet it or enjoy its company. Well, just bear with me on this one. It's not denial forever—I am suggesting a short-term strategy to make training easier and to help build up a healthy relationship with your dog.

Dogs love affection and touch. It's this natural desire for close pack association that I will be exploiting in all the dog-training exercises in this book. In fact, if you train three times daily as I advise, play games, and

Right:
We love petting and stroking our dogs. For the duration of this program, though, strokes and cuddles must be strictly rationed.

walk your dog in combination with the training, then the amount of attention, touch, and petting the dog receives will be quite considerable. Touch simply being linked to training and is no longer idle contact.

The Ignore

It's quite natural when people are relaxing in a room to see pet dogs occasionally walking up to someone for attention or a casual stroke. Stroking dogs is good for us, and the dogs certainly like it. Normally such displays of affection take place at the dog's instigation. To help training, we need to review these routines.

Unfortunately, from now on the rule is ignore it! No more sitting on laps and no more strokes or attention for free. I know it is hard and that you feel bad. Good! If you feel bad, you are probably following my advice really well. Remember, you will be able to offer your dog plenty of attention through the training exercises later.

Dog Training and the Leadership Program

By far the most useful and impressive way to be a leader is to train your dog, and the Leadership Program helps you to do this. Few dogs that are well trained and treated as dogs (rather than surrogate humans) cause any problematic behavior. Dogs that first understand what you want them to do and then obey all—not some—of your commands are showing you their lower position within the family pack and are less likely to challenge your leadership. Your ability to command and your dog's willingness to obey removes most disputes—that can only be beneficial to dog and owner alike and improve the quality of everyone's life.

Left: *"Don't look at me like that— I'm ignoring you." You must not give in and start stroking a dog that comes to you looking for attention.*

Duration Of The Program

Each year I place about 500 of my clients' dogs on this program, and many thousands more experience it through my films and television advice. Without exception, the clients excitedly tell me of the positive changes they observe in their dogs' behavior, and that's before they begin the actual dog training. They admonish their dogs very little, and the dogs seem so keen and obedient. Moreover, the dog's confidence improves, and it becomes calmer.

Once your dog has been fully trained to the standard you require, during the following months you can begin to relax some of the rules—especially those governing stroking, attention, and being in your company. You will have taught the dog obedience, which is a new language, and communication, which improves your relationship. Conflict is minimal, and harmony should reign. If your dog appears to be backtracking, you may have relaxed your

grip a bit too soon. This is especially likely with very dominant dogs of any size or breed. Dogs that are naturally lower ranking by nature are less problematic, and privileges can be reintroduced more rapidly

The Hook—A Restriction Program For the Demanding Dog

I referred earlier to the problems of dealing with dogs that are dominant by nature. The dominant dog poses particular problems of its own, and that is where the hook restriction program can be helpful. This section looks at the use of the hook.

Many people complain that they cannot control their dog when visitors arrive. Chaos reigns as they try to stop the dog from jumping up and knocking into the visitors. Of course, good obedience training will prevent most of this, but in the short term I also use

1 *When a visitor arrives and rings the doorbell, does your dog rush to the door and start barking like this? It's time to try using the hook.*

2 *Restrain your dog at the door by attaching the lead to its collar before opening the door.*

hook restriction training. It utilizes a sturdy metal hook that is attached to a metal baseplate that can be securely screwed to a wall. It's like a child's playpen without bars and certainly helps control boisterous dogs. It also prevents dogs from believing that they can inspect, pester, or impose on each and every friend or visitor who might frequent your home.

Equip yourself with a food toy (this is a hollow rubber dog toy that can be stuffed with food) and a hook fixed to a suitable wall or baseboard. I also use a chain lead about 3 feet (1 m) in length and attach it to the dog's collar (not a choke collar). (The length depends on the dog's size.) Every day place the dog on the hook by slipping the end of the lead over it and put a small quantity of its daily food allowance in the rubber toy. This teaches the dog to associate the restriction of being on the hook with the pleasure of gnawing away at the toy. Most dogs take issue with this new regime by barking and performing other antics, but I ignore the dog and release it only when it is calm. After about a week of this new system, most dogs gladly walk to the hook with you and accept the new training.

Once taught, hook restriction can be used as a safety measure if you have workers entering your home and you don't want your dog to get on the road. It's also good when the dog is overexcited or when people arrive and the dog won't leave them alone. In time the training should prove effective, and the dog will learn to go to the front door with you on or off a lead and obediently escort your friends into your home. On your command, it can then receive some praise from them and in the appropriate fashion.

3 *Drop the loop of the lead over the hook and give your dog a food-stuffed toy to occupy its attention.*

4 *Now you can enjoy your guest's company while also appreciating a placid dog.*

4 • Puppy Training

In this section I introduce you to some good tips for training puppies. We certainly need to be less formal in our training compared with how we teach adult dogs. Above all, we must be more patient with a puppy. On average, puppies become available at around eight weeks. Certainly don't accept a puppy older than this if you wish to have the best chance of socializing it into your lifestyle.

Above: Try to begin training when your puppy is no older than eight weeks and its character is still very malleable.

Don't aquire two puppies together, even though some breeders remark how wonderful this can be. It's not. It simply makes training much more difficult. The two puppies will form a little pack and constantly compete with one another. Their natural attention will not be focused on you. If you want two dogs, buy one first, fully train it to adulthood, and then bring in a second.

Personality

If you have aquired a puppy with a very strong character or one that exhibits quite dominant behavior, you can implement the Leadership Program described in the previous chapter, making sensible alterations when necessary to take the puppy's age into account. This will certainly help the dominant puppy to learn its place in your family pack. Puppies do not normally arrive with bad habits. They are just naturally inquisitive with their normal innate drives—you can quickly manipulate this curiosity to suit your training purposes and to help ensure the puppy's future stability and welfare. Ignore anyone who states that puppies should be trained when they are older. This is not the case. Puppies can—and do—learn from day one in your home.

Below: Puppies are devoid of malice or bad intent—they simply follow their inbuilt urges.

Below: *A squeaky toy is ideal for teaching a puppy simple recall lessons. Squeak the toy and encourage the puppy to run to you with cries of **"Come."** Learning is wrapped up in an enjoyable game.*

I suggest that you regard the puppy as you would a two-year-old child—innocent of all actions. It does not know guilt or malice. It is simply driven by basic instincts and the desire to fit in with its new pack, however nondoglike they appear. A puppy's concentration span can be quite short. So limit any lesson to maybe five minutes in duration—they are easily distracted and are physically incapable of maintaining the stay position for more than a few seconds. Until the puppy is about four months of age, concentrate on trying to reinforce the ideas and actions you want the puppy to learn and perform, rather than be overconcerned about exactness. The exceptions are mouthing (using its teeth on you) and chewing any item as this may be dangerous.

You should be opportunistic in your training methods. We normally introduce a puppy to toys to encourage mind-stimulating activity and to direct its energies and sense of inquisitiveness into play. Squeaky toys really excite many puppies as they seem to imitate the sounds of prey animals. I sometimes use the toy around the kitchen. When I want to teach the recall, I'll squeak the toy and command **"Come"** simultaneously and praise the puppy or reward it with a tidbit when it responds.

A puppy in the wild will seek face-to-face contact with an adult dog in order to solicit food that the mature dog will regurgitate. Despite the disparity in size between a puppy and its human owner, the puppy will still try to get to our mouths for regurgitation purposes. When they rush up to us, try holding the toy, a food tidbit, or just your outstretched fingers above the puppy. It will often fall into a sit position as it concentrates its vision on the focus point—as soon as this happens, give the command **"Sit"** and treat the puppy with a reward. I use the same motivational techniques to teach other disciplines, like the **"Down."**

Introduction Of The Lead And Collar

First attach the puppy's collar around its neck for a few days, so that it can get used to it. Initially the puppy may scratch it, as the collar feels unnatural. Next attach a 3- to 4-foot (1–1.2 m) lead to the collar. Don't try to walk the puppy as you would an adult dog. If you attempt to do this, the puppy is likely to panic as soon as the lead tightens and checks its movement in any direction. The best way is simply to fit the collar around the puppy's neck while sitting on the floor with a small bag of tidbits. When the puppy darts about, offer it a tidbit as a distraction. At some point it will run off to the full length of the lead and be brought to a halt. Take its mind off the sudden tightening of the lead by moving your arm to give the lead more slack while offering the puppy a tidbit as a distraction. Puppies quickly recover their sense of curiosity and will start playing again.

Next begin to walk about the room, offering the puppy tidbits or a toy while trying to keep the lead loose. Slowly the puppy will get used to the restriction caused by the collar and lead. If it suddenly darts off and the lead abruptly tightens, it may panic. Immediately drop the lead to release the tension and allow the puppy to drag the lead behind it. After a few seconds, pick up the lead again and continue training. A few minutes per session are all that is required, repeated perhaps five or six times daily. Practice the same routines in the yard. Only when the puppy is not fearful of the lead and collar should you attempt to walk in public places and begin heelwork training.

1 *Once you have habituated a puppy to wearing a collar, you can start to accustom it to walking on the lead.*

2 *Try to keep the lead loose as you walk the puppy around the room. A tightening of the lead on the collar can induce a sense of panic in a young dog.*

3 *Use tidbits or a toy to encourage the puppy to stick close by you. It will start to get the idea of walking to heel.*

TOILET TRAINING

During the first stage of housebreaking a puppy it is a good idea to restrict its access to the entire house. Install a large playpen in a chosen room with an easy-to-clean floor and line the room with newspapers. Put the puppy's pen with its bed in it in the room. Puppies need to relieve themselves on waking up and after each meal. At these times take your puppy outside for toilet training, and praise it when it empties its bowels or urinates. At other times, while in the room, the puppy has to relieve itself on the newspaper. Over time the puppy is conditioned to learn that it can either defecate or urinate outside in the yard or on the newspaper, and it will seek out one or other of these places when it needs them.

When the puppy is around 14 weeks old, remove the pen and reduce the newspapers until they cover about half the floor. Move the puppy's bed to a corner away from the papers. It should naturally use the reduced paper area to relieve itself when not taken outside for that purpose. Gradually the paper can be moved toward the door leading to the yard and finally outside (weighted down to stop it blowing away). A dog flap will also encourage a dog to go outside to urinate or defecate when it wants to. Remember to praise your puppy whenever it performs in the right place.

Once the puppy is relieving itself outside reliably, you can start to open up the rest of the house slowly for it to investigate. Remember to leave a small area of paper in the original room in case of emergencies.

Teaching Stay Positions

When teaching puppies to stay, use a lead and collar for control. You can hold the lead at any point to help control the pup's movements. Initially concentrate on teaching the puppy to stay for about five seconds and then step this up to around 30 seconds over a week or two while moving a few steps away. The length of time a puppy stays is not the important point—what you are trying to do is to instill the idea of the stay. Puppies find staying for long a little too much for their concentration levels. They tend to roll over, flop, and suddenly take off in a playful run. That is not disobedience; it's no different than a child being attracted to something else in its immediate world. Just persevere and congratulate yourself on succeeding when you manage to achieve small increments.

In the yard or park, I don't believe that puppies should be let off the lead to run free all the time. They must learn that it is normal for you to be in control. This is the time for the puppy, however young, to learn to concentrate on you. It only takes a few admirers to crouch down and let the puppy jump up at them for a stroke for the puppy to learn that jumping on people is very rewarding.

Simple Recall Training

I use a flexilead in the yard or park to begin recall training using the same methods as for adult dogs. Use inducements like food rewards to encourage your puppy to train. These will suffice in most cases. However, for the older puppy or one which is persistently reluctant to come for any rewards or is too keen on something it has stuck its little nose into, I tug the lead gently but just sufficiently to interrupt the puppy. This is not meant to hurt it or pull it back to me. When the puppy's head pops up to

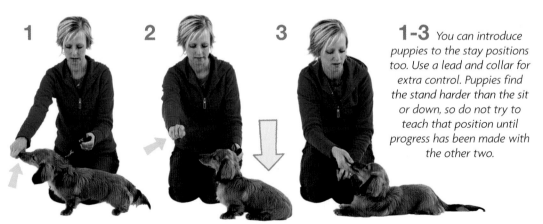

1 **2** **3**

1-3 *You can introduce puppies to the stay positions too. Use a lead and collar for extra control. Puppies find the stand harder than the sit or down, so do not try to teach that position until progress has been made with the other two.*

see what that was for, I quickly call it to me excitedly. Long lines or flexileads are very important when safety is required. Puppies will sometimes run off in pursuit of a dog in the park without thinking about you. Of course, use of the line use does not preclude using toys, food, and your own dramatic ability to attract your puppy's attention and encourage it to come to you. We are simply establishing early conditioning of the various lessons we want the puppy to learn in the future.

Right: Little food rewards help to teach a puppy the first stages of recall training.

Puppy Training Plan

Puppies should be taught the following exercises over approximately a five-minute period. Aim to repeat the training three or four times a day for a period of 21 days. You can use any of the methods marked Puppy Safe in the training section of the book.

WEEK 1	WEEK 2	WEEK 3
Sit	**Sit**	**Sit**
Down	**Down**	**Down**
Heel	**Heel**	**Heel**
Sit/Stay for about five seconds	**Sit/Stay** for up to 10 seconds	**Stand** introduction
Down/Stay for about five seconds	**Down/Stay** for up to 10 seconds	**Sit/Stay** for up to 20 seconds
Recall on a lead, several times	**Recall** on a flexi- or longer lead, several times	**Down/Stay** for up to 30 seconds
		Recall off lead in yard and around the house, several times

5 • *Communication*

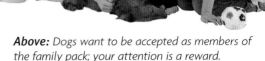

In order to explain more efficient ways of training your dog, it's necessary to understand something about a dog's psychology. Dogs do not reason as we do, and that fact alone can cause many problems in the owner-dog relationship. When a dog does something that you don't like, don't admonish it for an action that is past. Dogs, like little children, live for the moment. The past and future do not really come into the equation.

Dogs learn in a very black-and-white fashion and mainly by association. So if an action like teaching the dog to sit or go down produces a reward such as praise, food, or a pat, the dog will naturally wish to repeat that action. Conversely an unpleasant experience—perhaps the dog grabs some orange peel out of bin and is upset by its acidic taste—produces an immediately unrewarding experience.

Voice Tone

Different human voice tones attract different reactions from a dog. The dog's reaction will vary depending on how high or low the tone is. So it is important to limit your commands to a single syllable like **"No"** rather than a confusing jumble of words like "You bad dog, what have you done?" Command your dog in a crisp tone.

Rewards

Dogs like rewards. Appreciation of what they have achieved is not a concern for them, but keeping in favor with pack members and especially the higher-ranking ones is of

Above: *Dogs want to be accepted as members of the family pack; your attention is a reward.*

importance. Understand that a dog will seek out behavior that is rewarding for itself. Rewards given by you, the leader, include attention, verbal praise, physical touch, tasty food, time in your company, play with a toy, retrieve games, or any other action/response that gives the dog a feeling of being accepted by you.

Unrewarding Experiences

Punishment is the word often used for the unrewarding experiences that we use to help train dogs. It is not a term I like as to me it has a vengeful connotation and is not appropriate for dealing with dogs. However, for ease of reference in this book we may use the term punishment for simplicity's sake. Dogs want to avoid unpleasantness. They don't like being hurt or upset or rejected by the pack. We can use such unrewarding experiences to manipulate the dog's senses and modify its behavior by their use.

Direct punishment or an unrewarding experience can be many things. It may simply involve you ignoring the animal, rejecting its company. If the dog chews its lead, we can put a taste deterrent on it and that is truly unrewarding. Most of all, like the wolf, we can use vocalized threats in our own way— which is simply the word **"No."** What you will not find in this book is any suggestion that you can hit a dog to discourage bad behavior—that is not recommended, and we have other more effective ways of getting our way.

Timing

We have established that dogs will learn by associating any action that you are teaching it (in this case a training exercise) with a command backed up by a rewarding or unrewarding experience. How you go about this is crucial to how quickly the dog will learn. Timing is everything. Whether punishing or rewarding a dog, the reaction (the reward or punishment) has to be delivered at the time of the action or at least within two seconds of it for the dog to begin to make a link between the two.

Most novice dog handlers find it hard at first to combine the full set of dog-training skills—command, timing, and praise consistently delivered at the crucial moment. It's just a matter of practice—sometimes you should practice your skills on your own before bringing the dog into the equation.

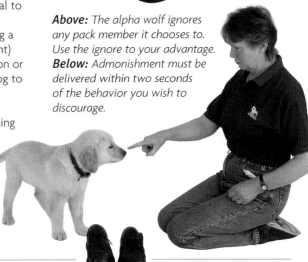

Above: The alpha wolf ignores any pack member it chooses to. Use the ignore to your advantage.
Below: Admonishment must be delivered within two seconds of the behavior you wish to discourage.

Hand Signals

Dogs are very observant and can spot movement, especially at a distance, very acutely. Close up they have poor eyesight compared to us. If you wish to add hand signals to complement your training commands, then this can be done as soon as your dog begins to follow your verbal commands consistently. Hand signals are just another link in the chain, like the whistle. Hands signals are very useful when the dog is at some distance from you.

I say hand signals, but dogs are masters of interpreting body language and so take far more from your physical training style than just the arm and hand movements. Dogs notice your whole physical demeanor—the way the body bends when you execute a **"Down"** command, for instance—and the entire body movement becomes the signal in time. The subtleties of a person's body actions are readily apparent to most dogs.

Now let's look at some pictures of the signals used in the basics of dog training so that you will understand the essential "vocabulary" that we shall use in the training program.

STAY

When putting your dog in any of the stay positions and then commanding **"Stay,"** the appropriate hand signal is the right hand used with the palm facing the dog with your arm fully outstretched. Start fairly close to the dog's face when moving away from the dog, and maintain the signal until you reach the desired distance.

DOWN

For the down position, your palm should be facing the ground level with your chest with your arm outstretched in front of you. Then make a clear downward movement to just below your waist.

SIT

Place your right palm facing the dog in an upright position, and then move your hand upward while maintaining the vertical position.

STAND

Using your right hand as if you are signaling a right turn, move your arm out from your hip so it extends to the right at shoulder level.

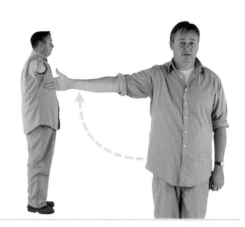

COME (RECALL)

First you must get your dog's attention. Once it is looking at you, extend your arm diagonally down toward the ground and bring your palm in toward your chest in a "gathering in" motion. Another option is to stretch out both arms with palms facing the dog at about waist height. As soon as you have the dog's attention, lower your bodily position so that you become more appealing to run to. The hands are then taken from the outstretched position down to about knee level and brought together in one clear movement.

6 • *Excessive Attention Seeking*

Before we begin the training plan, the next section of the book looks at a variety of problem behaviors and explains why they occur and what we can do to overcome them. We begin with excessive attention seeking.

Attention seeking—what does this actually mean? After all, most dogs are show-offs" who love attention. Dogs wouldn't be dogs unless they did. In fact dogs that seek our attention are the most trainable. Trainers develop a host of methods to attract a dog's attention in order to teach it obedience and sociable manners. However, when the attention-seeking dog interferes with your lifestyle, then this behavior becomes unacceptable.

From the day a puppy is born, it has an instinctive drive not only to survive but eventually to become pack leader. One of its tools is the ability to get attention. Dogs that demand your attention on cue, by order, by stealth or by looking dolefully into your eyes, get noticed. Dogs that get noticed succeed in life. That is why dogs seek our attention. So what's wrong with a bit of attention seeking? Well, the

Right: Most of us enjoy playtime with a dog. When pestering for attention starts to interfere with the normal running of your everyday life, you need to act.

main problem is that when we want our dogs' attention, it should be on our terms, not theirs.

Excessive attention seeking on your dog's terms means that the behavior is so over-developed that it is unbearable. You cannot go about your daily chores without tripping over the dog, which has already worked out yet another way of interrupting your routine, like sitting on your knee. Attention it definitely gets, which is, naturally, to its benefit.

Of course, the point at which attention seeking becomes a nuisance rather than a pleasure depends on your character as well as the dog's. Some people simply love and encourage their dog's attention as it makes them feel needed and loved. In this case, it actually adds to their sense of well-being—and to their dog's likewise. However, in other cases, the dog's attention seeking has a distinctly negative effect, disrupting the owner's lifestyle. At that point, the dog/human relationship is on the rocks.

The majority of dogs presented to me for excessive attention seeking are in fact the toy breeds like Yorkies or Pekingese. Their small size makes it very tempting to pick them up and cuddle them all the time, with the result that they become overattached and never learn to stand on their own feet. Problems are also common with insecure rescue dogs. Here the temptation is to compensate for their

Don't shout at a dog behaving like this; it may interpret that as a reward.

Above: *A large dog in your lap is about the last thing you want. The best response is to stand up immediately while avoiding eye contact with the dog.*

attention department. The rules of the pack are simple: use your brain to get what you want and when you want it. The only way this can be stopped is by a smarter, more consistent fellow pack member—you—acting like a higher-ranking and more dominant dog. If you have problems with your dog's behavior, then you have to act like the boss all of the time. The end result will be your dog changing into a well-behaved companion—and moreover a dog that loves and respects you even more because you are an excellent pack leader. Strong leaders lead: they do not fawn over the pack members.

Below: *Toy breeds in particular can develop attention-seeking strategies to an undesirable degree.*

poor start in life by lavishing attention on them—only to find that the more you give, the more the dog demands.

Tackling The Problem

So what's going on? Dominance is what's going on, or, to be more specific, passive dominance—a helplessness that demands attention from owners and friends. These dogs basically want to become top dog in the

Excessive Attention Seeking

What Is Excessive?

While there's little doubt that this behavior problem is learned, there is a lot of difference of opinion as to what is excessive. What one owner thinks is much too much may be quite acceptable to another. Inconsistencies can also occur within families, causing variations in reaction that simply confuse a dog and make it more difficult to alter the behavior.

This happens when some visitors encourage your dog's advances with rewards (touch, praise, rough play) while other visitors lose their cool at the sight of a single dog hair on their clothes.

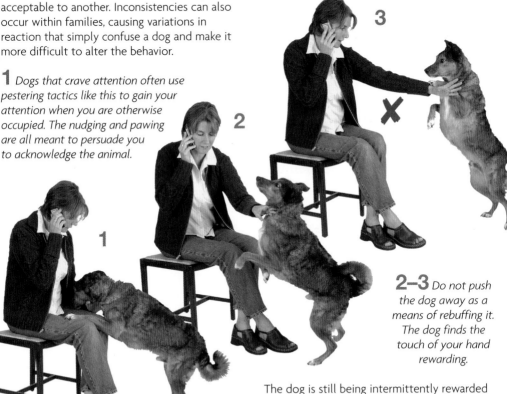

1 *Dogs that crave attention often use pestering tactics like this to gain your attention when you are otherwise occupied. The nudging and pawing are all meant to persuade you to acknowledge the animal.*

2–3 *Do not push the dog away as a means of rebuffing it. The dog finds the touch of your hand rewarding.*

The dog is still being intermittently rewarded and so will continue to try to solicit more attention until all visitors ignore its advances— and continue to do so until the behavior ceases to be a problem. This may even mean your leading the dog into the house on a collar and lead and popping the end of the lead over a hook or fixture to keep it at bay until it has calmed down after visitors have arrived.

Of course, most dogs work by stealth—especially when you are on your own. Many owners fall into the trap of petting their dog whenever it seeks attention. When they think they have shown it enough attention, they stop and expect the dog to understand that they have been fair. It doesn't. All it knows is that it can demand attention with a fair degree of success. So pat your dog only when petting is initiated by you. At all other times, ignore it.

Many crafty dogs bring toys for you to throw. Don't be deceived. This looks clever, but it is just another ploy that the dog has learned to control you and get attention. Don't respond at all. Keep your hands still and your mouth shut, and wait until your dog becomes bored and goes away. Then maybe later, get the toy, throw it, and make the dog bring and release it. When the game is over, put the toy away. Again your dog will see you behaving like the boss and respect you for it. In time it can still have fun on your (not its) terms, and eventually its pestering tactics will cease.

How To Prevent Attention Seeking

Teach your dog that spending time on its own is normal—see some of the tips on tackling separation anxiety on pages 54–57. Build up gradually from five minutes to one hour twice daily, over several weeks. Whenever your dog

nudges you or looks at you with doleful eyes, ignore it completely. Even if it starts crawling over you, which is unlikely, don't push it off as the mere physical touch can be construed by the dog as a reward.

Moreover remember that to **ignore** the dog is your best training device. In the short term, if a dog is impossible and you find ignoring it very difficult, then using some deterrent spray on your person or your seating area will deter it from coming near you. Orange or lemon peel rubbed on your hands may discourage the endless nudging with which some dogs seek attention. Large, powerful dogs that literally throw themselves at you may need a set of training disks to dissuade them from bullying you into giving them attention—but don't use these on very sensitive dogs or young puppies.

Taking Control

• Ignore attention-seeking approaches— the message is "Don't tell me when to stroke you."
• Use deterrent spray on your chair— "Don't approach my seat."
• Rub orange or lemon peel on your hands— "Don't nudge me."
• Use training disks or a deterrent spray— under expert guidance.
• Remember that friends and family must treat the dog in the same way. Consistency is important.

7 • *Jumping Up*

Dogs seem to be obsessed with face-to-face contact, wanting to lick and nudge our faces and mouths with theirs. Between dogs this is an important social action, serving as a greeting, a plea for an older dog to regurgitate food, and even a sign of submission. When it's directed at a human, the height difference means that they learn to jump up to reach our faces. This is a nuisance, and it can also be dangerous, especially when big dogs and small children or elderly people are involved.

Like most habits, this one starts in puppyhood. Puppies are small, so we naturally bend down or lift them up, giving them the perfect opportunity to lick our faces. As the puppy grows, it naturally tries to continue this behavior by jumping toward our faces.

Right: Try not to allow a puppy to lick the faces of family members.

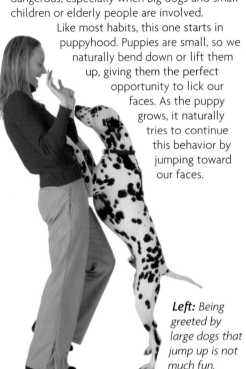

Left: Being greeted by large dogs that jump up is not much fun.

Four Paws on the Ground

If you have a puppy don't allow it to lick faces, especially where children are involved. When you greet your dog, command **"Sit,"** and offer praise only when your puppy has all four paws on the ground. If it does jump up, stand absolutely still and say nothing. To the puppy this is boring, and it will quickly learn that there's no fun or reward to be had by jumping up. All the family and any visitors must participate in this program consistently if the behavior is to be stopped.

Owners often try to deter their dog by hitting it or pushing it off, to no avail. Unfortunately, for most dogs any kind of touch is a strong reward, so they can interpret what is intended as a corrective measure as encouragement—a rough kind of game. Over time, the dog's resistance to its owner's efforts builds up, wearing the owner down and toughening up the dog.

Initial Triggers That Teach Dogs To Jump Up

When we are sitting down and a little puppy jumps up, placing its front paws on our knees, it's a natural response to lean forward (trigger 1) and either stroke the puppy (trigger 2) or, even worse, lift it on to our lap for a cuddle (trigger 3). Three reinforcements have taken place, laying the foundations for a dog that jumps up in the future. Even if you then put the dog back on the floor, it has learned an important association: jumping up brings rewards. Dogs that are lifted onto a lap obviously enjoy the contact, but it's unfair to do this with a puppy and expect it to understand when it is bigger that you no longer want it on your knees. It's even more confusing to the puppy if you let it jump on you but not on your friends. Dogs need black-and-white rules. Teach what you want for the long term, not for the immediate moment.

Playing with the puppy on the floor may be wiser. Such play is far more interactive and coincidentally removes the puppie's need or wish to jump up.

I'm Home, I'm Ignoring You

Many readers will have dogs who are already expert at jumping up and getting their own way. Now let's look at some methods to counter a dog's expertise. Aim to eliminate whatever excites the jumping up. For example, if your dog jumps up when you return home, then stop greeting it when you come in. At each homecoming ignore it for the first 15 minutes. Keep your hands still, and don't even say hello. Ensure that all family members do the same. Your dog should soon learn that there's no point in continuing to jump up. After the first 15 minutes, you can call the dog to you, tell it to sit, and give a reward that does not overexcite it. You have now simply reorganized the time and manner of greeting to suit you. Dogs adapt with no hard feelings.

Left: The ignore response is a powerful deterrent to stop this type of behavior. The dog is deprived of any touch or voice reward when it pesters you on its hind legs.

Jumping Up

Dog Training

Obedience training, combined with the ignore exercise, has the highest chance of success. If you train your dog to a high standard, then you'll have a dog that listens to your commands. If your dog learns to sit on command, whenever it's about to jump up, instruct **"Sit."** When it sits, praise it verbally. Make sure that jumping up is always ignored, never rewarded. Once it realizes that, it will soon try sitting to achieve the desired praise. Remember, though, that consistency is vital.

Redirect Unwanted Greetings

If your dog loves retrieving games with toys or balls, then take one with you to the park. For the first ten lessons, make sure the dog does not have access to any of its retrieve toys at home. As soon as you see your dog about to pay unwanted attention to a passerby, call the dog and throw its ball or toy. This is a good distraction method for dogs that like retrieving. Timing is vital, so attract your dog's attention before it jumps on someone, not afterward. Using a whistle to signify a game helps to get the dog's attention before you throw the toy.

Water and Sound Deterrents

(for determined and dominant dogs only)
This method is best suited to dogs that have long-established jumping-up problems, very big dogs that can hurt people by jumping up, and dogs that need to be retrained quickly because

Above: *Obedience-trained dogs can be briskly commanded to sit when they start to jump up in an unwelcome way. The verbal praise—**"Good dog"**—should come only when it is sitting.*

children or old people are involved. You will need a water pistol or a dog repellent sound alarm.

If the dog jumps up when you return home, have the water pistol by the door. As you come in and see it about to jump up, command **"No"** and squirt water in its face. Repeat this as many times as needed to stop the dog. Eventually it will come to associate jumping up with an unpleasant squirt of water, and this will discourage the bad habit. Some dogs find an alarm more offputting than a water pistol.

Smell and Taste Deterrents
(for determined and dominant dogs only)
Bitter apple and other safe, nontoxic dog repellent scents are also useful to dissuade dogs from jumping upon us. I find this especially helpful with children or the elderly. If the dog jumps up on the child when you are nearby, spray the air around the dog (or the child can do this itself if he or she is old enough to follow instructions). The dog discovers that instead of the reward of being fondled or even pushed away, it has the unpleasant experience of reaching toward a target that stinks. This interrupts its learned behavior pattern. Most dogs learn quickly that jumping up is no longer enjoyable, as long as the humans involved act consistently.

Collar, Lead, and Hook
Most dogs are highly conditioned to the collar and lead, which has pleasant associations for them. Your dog will normally be happy to allow you to connect its lead and will follow you.

This conditioning can be used to control dogs jumping up at visitors in the home. Hang the lead on an easily accessible hook, on a wall, or near the front door. When the visitor arrives, as the dog starts jumping about excitedly, clip its lead on, then choose one of the next steps, depending on your level of control.

1 Tell the dog to sit well away from the door. If it jumps up at the visitor, snap the lead and command **"No"**. Now make it heel as you escort the visitor into your house. If the dog has calmed down, drop the lead on the floor, but leave it attached in case you need to exercise further control. After about 15 minutes, if all is well, disconnect the lead. Make sure the visitor does not fuss over the dog to excite it again.

2 If the dog is uncontrollable, then connect it to a hook on the wall and attach the lead to it for about 15 minutes. Release it only if it calms down, and ask the visitor to ignore the dog initially.

Left: A sudden squirt with a water pistol or plant spray is an effective deterrent that will take even large, pushy dogs by surprise.

8 • Play Biting

When puppies leave the litter and arrive in our homes, they bring with them their experiences, one of which is using their mouth—play biting, mouthing, nibbling, and play growling. Investigative mouthing behavior is exhibited at a very young age in puppies for a number of different reasons. Though the teeth are for eating food, another use is to help littermates learn bite inhibition and how much pressure to use on one another. Sharp puppy teeth hurt, without causing real damage. So when a litter of puppies are play fighting, they quickly learn how hard they can bite without upsetting a playmate. However, when humans take the place of littermates, puppies can become confused. Without correct training, continued mouthing can develop into habitual

play biting. Though it is termed "play," what we are really talking about is dogs and puppies actually biting people, which hurts!

A common scenario occurs when a puppy wishes to initiate play or attention. The puppy nips the owner who reacts, either by pushing the puppy away—which it interprets as joining in the game—or by encouraging rough play games. Either way, the puppy learns that play biting is acceptable. Early dominance behavior like growling or snapping can also be a problem, though this is less common in very young puppies. Whatever is happening, the dog should be discouraged and stopped swiftly.

Most people genuinely don't like being bitten, in fun or otherwise. Unfortunately when nipped, we naturally recoil. Children especially react in a defensive manner, which encourages the puppy (or dog). Instead of learning not to bite, it learns to bite more. As time goes on the puppy can become even more dominant and it finds this behavior rewarding. It bites, you pull your hand or clothing away, and then a tug-of-war ensues, which is even more fun.

Eventually the puppy or adolescent dog learns that in this contest it is dominant—it normally wins the game, and that's what being a dog is all about. As the dog gets rougher, the owner's shouting and aggression increase—all very rewarding in terms of canine play. By this stage, of course, young children are hopelessly unable to deal with the dog and also begin to avoid its rough play biting. Unfortunately, the dog has now been conditioned to play bite.

Above: Puppies use their teeth and mouths to investigate the world about them.

Left: Don't allow any games that involve play biting.

What's Behind The Habit?

• Play biting among puppies helps to establish bite inhibition—a sense of how hard they can bite without causing real injury.
• Among themselves, puppies deter rough play bites by biting back. They also deter this behavior by refusing to play with the biter—and this is a useful tip.

Shutting the dog in another room only makes it frustrated, hyperactive, and keener than ever to enjoy its dominant playtime.

Toy or Prey

Many toys on the market are designed for human/dog fun, such as tough fabric ropes made for tug-of-war games. They are safe when used with a strict set of rules—notably that the owner always wins and that the dog allows you, on command, to take the toy away at any time without a fight or any grumbling. Thousands of dogs enjoy the exercise and the mind-stimulating game, and so do their owners. However, it is inadvisable to allow children under the age of twelve to play tug-of-war with dogs unless supervised and important to insist

that they play by the rules above. If you notice the dog beginning to growl and becoming overstimulated and aggressive, take that as your signal to end that type of tug-of-war game, maybe for good.

Below: Take care when playing tug-of-war games with a dog. You must always win and keep control over the toy.

Play Biting

Remedial Action

This advice applies mostly to puppies but is also worth using with any newly acquired adult dog. From day one, avoid playing any games which involve mouthing, i.e., teeth on skin. If your puppy tries to solicit attention from you by play biting, ignore it. Just get up and walk away. Alternatively, take hold of the puppy by the scruff and say **"No"** sharply, looking directly into its eyes for about two seconds. Then let the dog go and ignore it. This is normally enough to discourage play biting in the very early stages, say between six and 18 weeks, and it teaches your puppy the useful **"No"** command. If the puppy or young dog has already developed play biting to a high degree, then holding the scruff may be seen by the dog as more rough play or a dominant threat, so it

is best just to say **"No"** and then ignore it.

With an adult dog, leaving a lead trailing behind it—only when you are present—is also an excellent method to stop determined play biters. By grabbing the lead you automatically get instant control—you can drop the lead end on to a wall hook or doorknob, and instantly the dog is prevented from continuing its play biting when you move out of its reach. Alternatively, with large dogs (not puppies), you can check the dog with the lead, giving maybe four or five checks within as many seconds. The point is not to hurt the dog's neck but to interrupt the undesirable action. If the dog begins again, I simply repeat the rapid check but always accompanied with the command **"No."** I will then drop the lead and continue with whatever I was doing. If the dog begins again, I repeat the rapid check.

By using the lead and collar, you are not touching the dog's body, which reduces any contact that the dog might take as rough play or reward. Never hit out with your hand or have a screaming

Below: Ignore a dog that play bites to gain your attention.

Left and below: *Attach a lead to an adult dog that play bites. It allows you to gain control and bring hook restriction (see p. 26) into the equation.*

match with your dog. Dogs are faster than we are and therefore simply enjoy the game of "I play bite, you hit out and miss, I dive in again".

Dog Training

The traditional (and still the best) way to prevent or stop play biting is to obedience train your dog. Puppies should be trained from six weeks onward (see pages 28–33). Concentrate on the **"Down, stay"** position. When this has been mastered, you can command your dog to do this when it tries to play bite. This is time-consuming. Once you have put in the work, you will enjoy your dog's company more.

Redirecting the Play

Throwing a toy or a ball is another distraction method that I use. Squeaky toys are ideal. Directing the dog's attention to a toy instead of your hand is a very safe and effective way of reducing

play biting and, at the same time, teaching the dog what it can use its teeth on.

Some dogs mouth their owner's hand when being walked. If your dog grabs your hand while you are holding the lead, snap the lead sharply, ignore the dog and carry on walking as if nothing has happened. Don't give the dog any attention at all. If you react like this consistently, your dog will find mouthing your hand not much fun. You can also try using a deterrent spray. Spray your hand and the lead just before embarking on the walk. Taste deterrents work on most dogs, especially if used for many weeks to ensure that the lesson is well implanted. In the home your dog may be an armchair mouther, constantly reaching for your hand when you are sitting down. Again, a deterrent spray applied to your hand each time you settle down will discourage this behavior.

Left: *If your dog mouths your hand when walking, spray the lead and your hand with a bitter spray as a deterrent.*

9 • *Stealing Food*

Dogs are scavengers by nature. Wild dogs owe their success to their virtually omnivorous eating habits and their readiness to supplement hunting kills by eating carrion and anything else they find. To a wild dog, any food source can mean the difference between life and death. Domestic dogs have their food supplied by us, but they retain the instinct not to waste anything—whether it be an unguarded sandwich in the house or animal droppings in the park.

Food is the strongest driving force for animals in the natural world. Domestic dogs are fed on a regular basis, but they still have the urge to supplement this occasionally with what they find. This is frequently provided by neglectful humans who leave cakes, sandwiches, cookies, and other delights on temptingly low tables. It would be unnatural for a dog to turn from such an opportunity. Each successful foray reinforces the dog's instinct to hunt down such supplementary snacks.

Often, dogs learn to steal food more out of boredom than from hunger. Dogs that have been left for long periods of time with little stimulation seek to entertain themselves, just as we would if we were stuck in a room for too long on our own. Their acute sense of smell encourages them to explore, and the exciting aromas escaping from the kitchen trash can are irresistible. Tipping over the trash can not only provides a food reward but also fun rummaging and investigating. Having found the experience rewarding, a dog is likely to repeat it. To prevent this, secure all trash cans, indoors and outdoors.

Obedience Training

At home or in the park, teaching your dog to obey your obedience commands is the only sure way to prevent scavenging. Since dogs cannot understand our views on food, they need to be taught that **"No"** means **"No"** and not "Maybe." It's advisable to teach puppies or new adult dogs the word **"No"** early on. Then walk your dog around the house on collar and lead. If it approaches any food, check it with the lead and tell it **"No."** Leave food out in a container that allows it to be seen and smelled but that prevents the dog from getting a reward if it snatches the food. This is vital, as one food reward may be remembered by an opportunistic dog forever.

The rules are made clearer to your dog if you never hand-feed it and never offer it food from your plate. Few dogs waste their efforts staring and drooling at the plates of people who never feed them by hand. It's natural to hand your dog a portion of what you are eating as a way of saying, "Let's share but don't take." However, what this signals to the dog is that whenever you have food there is always a chance of a reward, and this simply increases the likelihood that it will start helping itself.

Deterrents

In my experience, deterrents are less effective than prevention. Some people recommend discouraging theft by leaving out food smeared with an unpleasant-tasting substance, such as mustard. This is usually a waste of time. Most dogs smell the horrible potion and steer well clear of it but still continue to steal untreated food. Others will just eat anything and look for seconds—treated or untreated.

Below: Where there's a will, there's a way. Dogs can smell food from far away and will eat what they find unguarded, unless they are trained not to do so.

Above: In the wild, dogs are programmed not to waste food, so we shouldn't be too surprised when this happens!

Stealing Food

Prevention Advice

Dogs develop the habit of taking food from tables or kitchen surfaces because of careless owners. One successful foray is all that's needed to establish the practice. The best prevention is never to leave food unattended. Lock away every tempting morsel. This will eliminate the reward and stop the habit from developing—especially in the puppy and adolescent periods, when bad habits are easily formed.

Left: Do not accustom your dog to receiving tidbits from your food plate. You risk setting up a situation where it expects hand-fed treats all the time.

With a dog already conditioned to stealing, set up the dog regularly (see page 53) so that you control the situation and are not caught off guard. Allowing the dog to dictate the agenda is a recipe for failure. You must be in control at all times.

Below: With young children around, scraps of food often find their way onto the floor. Keep your dog out while a child is feeding.

The combination of young children, food, and dogs can be a nightmare for you—and a delight for most dogs. Toddlers often rain food down on dogs from their high chairs, and this is a difficult situation to resolve. Probably the best solution is to keep your dog out of the room while the child is eating and not let it back in until you have cleaned up all crumbs and splatters. If the dog has learned the **"No"** command, you can use this to restrain it. Alternatively, you can use the hook restriction method described on pages 26–27.

Direct Action

When your dog steals food in your presence, the **"No"** command can be backed up with various aids, such as a water pistol or training disks. As it reaches for the food, squirt water at its face or throw training disks (or a large

*Below: Training disks can be effective in backing up the **"No"** command and teaching a dog that it must not steal from an unattended plate.*

Setting Up Your Dog

This "natural learning" method often has the best chance of teaching a dog what is a bad deal and what is a good deal in life. If you wish to dissuade your dog from stealing food when you are out of the room, then set it up. Tie several empty metal cans (make sure there are no sharp edges) together with string, secure the other end of the string to a piece of food such as a tough piece of meat, and place them all on a kitchen counter. Then leave the room. When your dog grabs the meat, it will pull off the cans, causing a terrible clatter.

Most dogs will be put off by the noise. Repeat the exercise regularly, with some variations and in different rooms. A dog will soon learn not to take food unless it is in the dog bowl.

Using Muzzles

In extreme cases where a dog constantly takes food (especially in the street or park where it may pick up dangerous substances), a muzzle may be necessary. Once a dog is accustomed to wearing the muzzle, it can go out anywhere without being able to scavenge. This interrupts the behavior pattern. Eventually, if this is combined with obedience training, it may learn not to eat what it finds. The muzzle can be used in the home for particularly persistent dogs or big strong dogs that are difficult to manage. Muzzles should not be left on dogs for more than two hours at a time and preferably less than that.

bunch of keys) just behind the dog. The squirt or the clattering noise will put off all but the most hardened thieves. Alternatively, you can use a remote-controlled spray deterrent collar (see page 192). The device is very effective in interrupting undesired behavior like stealing food, although you will need to learn from a trainer how to use it correctly.

10 • Separation Anxiety

Dogs and people love each other's company, and that is the reason most of us own dogs. Dogs are gregarious by nature and unsuited to leading solitary lives. From a dog's point of view, we are the family pack. Whether it lives with one person or a large family, it instinctively enjoys, and needs, our company. Leaving a dog alone regularly for long periods is not kind and does not equate with responsible dog ownership. However, dogs can adapt to spending reasonable stretches of time in their own company without suffering severe psychological problems.

For most well-adjusted dogs, anxieties rarely develop to the point of causing problem behavior. However, some dog owners find that leaving their beloved pet dog for even a short time can lead to difficulties. Reactions to being left alone include barking, howling, self-mutilation, excessively boisterous behavior on the owner's return, destructiveness, and even biting the owner as he or she leaves the house. All are caused by stress and come under the heading of separation anxiety.

General Causes

This problem nearly always arises when a puppy is spoiled or not conditioned to accept an appropriate routine. As a youngster, it may have been allowed to sleep in its owner's bedroom and received constant attention. The dog thinks it has a right to demand attention whenever it wishes. So if you respond to a dog every time it blinks its doleful eyes at you, you could have a separation anxiety problem in the making.

Dogs that go everywhere with their owners, day and night, can also turn out to be owner dependent. Understandably, therefore, separation

Above: Displays of destructiveness while left alone are typical of dogs that suffer from separation anxiety.

anxiety is more common in single-person households, especially when elderly people live alone with a dog as their sole companion. If only you and the dog occupy a house, then naturally you will be together most of the time. There are measures you can take to teach your dog to be self-sufficient, without forfeiting a close and rewarding relationship.

Too much pampering may cause a dog to become over-reliant on its owner.

Are You The Problem?

I would argue that dogs are blameless and that we are always the problem. I have been dealing with dogs and their owners for very many years, and this has taught me a great deal about the complex ways that we condition our dogs for our own psychological comfort and needs. We are not usually aware of this, but in some cases this interdependence can develop to an unhealthy level. If circumstances change

Causes in Brief

• Dogs have not learned from puppyhood to spend time alone but are given free run of the home with human company in all rooms.

• Some owners coddle their dogs excessively, often to satisfy their own emotional needs, thereby teaching the dogs to be helpless.

• Some dogs learn to be wholly human orientated, ignoring their own kind, which causes imbalance and insecurity.

• Small, cuddly breeds tend to attract excessive human attention, so separation anxiety is more common among toy breeds.

suddenly—for example, if we acquire a new spouse or a different job—and the dog is no longer needed as much, then it may react badly and develop separation anxiety.

Insecure dogs often want attention and company on demand, which compounds the separation anxiety problem. When you comply with your dog's demands, it comes to expect attention every time it asks, until the habit becomes firmly embedded. When there isn't enough attention, i.e., when you are not around, then separation anxiety may occur. You may observe excessive excitability and even shaking and shivering prior to your leaving. Once you've gone, barking and destruction may follow.

Separation Anxiety

Prevention Advice

The ideal solution is prevention. If you have a puppy or a new dog, teach it that it will be left alone for periods of half an hour to an hour several times a day—and for longer at night. This should be done gradually, starting with five minutes per session. Teach your puppy that it has its own area (or pen or cage) where you will visit it. Do not give the dog access to your whole house. If the puppy starts to cry when it's alone in its pen, wait until a silence occurs, then go in and make a mild fuss but not too much, otherwise you may encourage separation anxiety. Don't let the dog think that every time you come to its area it will be let out; sometimes leave the dog in and sometimes let it out. In other words, be unpredictable, in order to avoid setting up expectations.

Dealing With Separation Anxiety— Reducing Dependence

If possible, start this program during a long weekend. Begin by reducing the amount of attention your dog receives during a 24-hour period to 25 percent of what it was. Ignore all the dog's attempts to solicit attention, whether by nudging you, bringing toys, or looking pleadingly for a pat. You'll find this hard at first, but you and all your family and friends must be consistent.

Next, start leaving your dog on its own in a room of the house for periods of five minutes while you are still in the house. If the dog begins to cry, bark, or sound excited, don't go into the room. When a gap in the barking

Right: Ignore your dog when it paws and pesters you for attention. You need to work to reduce its sense of dependence on you.

comes, wait 30 seconds. Then go in casually, saying nothing and keeping the contact low-key. Then putter about for a few minutes and let the dog go free in the house. Ensure that no one pats the dog, no matter how much it solicits praise. The dog's initial puzzlement or even worse behavior will soon give way to acceptance of the new arrangements after a few days.

If this regimen is adhered to, the dog slowly learns that being with you or without you is no big deal. You should aim to leave your dog alone for five-minute periods, working up to four to six times a day. When this is achieved without any commotion, slowly begin increasing the period your dog spends alone up to the desired time to fit in with your social patterns.

The Use of Food

Using food rewards to modify your dog's behavior produces positive associations with your absence. The most useful aid is a tough rubber toy designed to be stuffed with food, which the dog has to pull out bit by bit. Instead of gulping its dinner down in a flash, it has a time-consuming but rewarding new hobby.

• Keep your dog in the kitchen area when you are out.

• Change its diet to a chemical- and additive-free food (no dry food).

• Feed your dog its daily dinner only through the toy.

• If you are out three times in one day, split the day's ration into three portions.

• Use the toy and stuff it with food when you are about to leave your dog. Place the toy on the kitchen floor and let the dog work on

Below: A food toy is a good way of teaching a dog to feel comfortable about spending time without human company. While it is absorbed in trying to extract its food from the toy, it is not concerned by your absence.

extracting the food each time it is placed on the floor.

• You can still use this method even if you are not going out. Leave the dog in the kitchen three times daily for about 15 minutes. Each time leave it the toy with a portion of its dinner inside. This will accustom the dog to positive rewards when you are out of the room, even though you may still be present in the house.

• Do not feed your dog or give it tidbits at any other time. All food must be fed through the toy.

• If your dog does not consume the food in the toy, place the whole thing in a plastic container in the fridge until the next lesson. Very few dogs will ignore the food in the toy by the second day.

Separation Anxiety

Exercise The Energy

Try lengthening your dog's exercise periods prior to leaving it alone, and make more effort to tire it out. Throw a ball and run around, or let your dog play with other friendly dogs. Don't just go for a lethargic stroll. Then, when you arrive home, leave your dog on its own for a while. If it's tired, it's much more likely to settle down and go to sleep. As in the previous method, gradually build up the time that you leave your dog alone.

During walks and exercise, you can praise and touch your dog as much as you like, especially when obedience training it. While you are working on dealing with separation anxiety, you will usually find as a bonus that your dog becomes far more obedient in the house and the park.

Right: This is classic ignore— no eye contact, arms folded, no pats or strokes. The dog already seems to realize that it's not getting anywhere.

Important Tips

1 Do not allow your dog to decide when attention should be forthcoming. Let any attention be on your terms. You decide when enough is enough. So for the next few months, always ignore your dog if it requests attention.

Below: Dogs that are tired after a stimulating period of exercise are more likely to settle down and go to sleep if they are then left on their own in the house.

Above: Play strenuous retrieve games to get your dog running good and hard.

2 If the anxiety is triggered by your leaving the house, then pretend to leave several times a day. Go through all the motions, including putting on your coat and going to your car. With so many false starts to contend with, your dog won't be able to predict when you are leaving, and this should disrupt the ingrained anxiety behavior.

3 Whenever you return home or when your dog has been in another room on its own for a while, don't greet it effusively or over-excite it. Instead, adopt a low-key approach. In this way your dog will not look upon your return as a big deal. Better still, ignore the dog completely for the first five minutes.

4 Remember that many dogs that crave attention consider being pushed off or reprimanded as a form of reward. So simply stand upright with your hands at your side if your dog jumps on you. Pause, then sit down again. Repeat until the dog loses interest. Don't give the dog any eye contact .

I have found that most dogs respond well to the above methods and that eventually you can reinstate a moderate amount of affectionate

response—in other words a relationship that both of you still enjoy. However, a few dogs are so conditioned to effusive displays of affection from their owners that praise and fuss always have to be kept to a minimum to prevent the dog's anxiety from becoming unbearable again.

Left: If your dog gets anxious when you are about to leave the house, make a series of false starts to confuse its expectations and so alleviate its anxiety.

Recap

• Use food rewards (the daily ration given via the food-stuffed toy) so the dog develops pleasant associations with separation from you.
• Teach your dog to be alone, initially for short periods.
• Tidbits given at other times are not helpful in solving this problem.
• Some dogs like a chew when alone.
• Don't allow your dog treats (including toys) when in your company, except when out on walks.

11 • *Excessive Barking*

There are several reasons why dogs may indulge in excessive barking or howling. Some owners encourage a puppy to bark to develop its guarding ability. In other cases, the owners have unintentionally encouraged it to bark from puppyhood. Whenever the dog barked, its owners appeared and gave it attention. By finding this behavior rewarding,

Right: *Dogs that bark too much can cause social and domestic tension.*

the dog quite naturally continued to bark more and more. This is especially true of puppies.

Some dogs bark from stress when separated from their owners. Others bark from boredom when they don't have enough stimulation. A dog whose routine is changed so that its owner can't spend as much time with it as usual may become frustrated and anxious—this is another cause of excessive barking or related problem behavior.

Prevention Advice For Puppies

The ideal solution is prevention. If you have a puppy or a new dog, teach it that being left alone for periods of half an hour to an hour several times a day, and for longer at night is normal. This should be done gradually, starting with five- to ten-minute periods. Also teach your puppy that it has its own cage, pen, or area where you will visit it. Don't, as a norm, give it access to your whole home. If, while the puppy is alone in its pen, it starts to cry, then wait until a silence occurs before going in and making a mild fuss over it. Verbal praise is sufficient, but not too much—otherwise you may encourage the barking.

Dogs naturally bark when visitors knock or ring the doorbell. Most owners don't mind this—territorial guarding is natural dog behavior. Don't let the dog overdo it, otherwise you could end up with an excessive barker. Most dogs that drive their owners crazy by barking at the door were taught when to bark but not when to stop.

Below: If you teach your puppy that spending time on its own in a crate or pen away from the family is normal, you reduce the chance that the dog will start barking excessively later in its life.

follow the Leadership Program (see pages 20–27), and read the section on separation anxiety (see pages 54–59) for more advice.

How To Stop or Reduce Barking

If possible start this program during a holiday or long weekend. Begin by reducing the amount of attention the dog receives during a 24-hour period. Ignore all the dog's attempts to solicit attention, whether nudging you, begging you to bring toys, or just looking for a pat. You'll find this hard at first, but you and all your family and friends must be consistent.

Then start leaving the dog on its own in a room of the house for periods of five minutes while you're still in the house. If the dog begins to bark, do not go into the room. When a gap in the barking comes, wait 30 seconds, then nonchalantly wander in and say hello, but keep the praise low key. Bursts of excitement from the dog should never be reciprocated. Then putter about for a few minutes and let the dog go free in the house. Ensure that no one pets the dog, no matter how much it solicits praise.

If this regimen is adhered to, the dog slowly learns that being with you or without you is no big deal. You should aim to leave your dog alone for five- to 15-minute periods five times daily. When this is achieved without barking, then slowly begin increasing the period that your dog spends alone, building up to the desired time.

Barking While the Owner Is Home

Some dogs don't like being left alone in the yard or in an adjacent room and, as a result, bark until the owner attends to their needs, which normally means giving the dog access to human company again. What a powerful reward! If your dog is this type of barker, then

Excessive Barking

Anxiety-Related Barking

Many dogs are overattached to their owners and appear to be incapable of spending time on their own. Use the following methods on such dogs to change their view of spending time alone. Food is on a dog's mind most of the time. If food is not, then we can easily induce it to think food, or at least make dinnertime more exciting. Always use natural dog food for this program. Avoid dry foods and any foods containing additives, which might influence your dog's behavior.

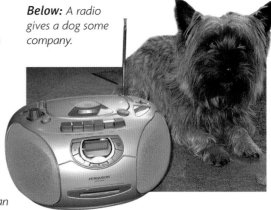

Below: A radio gives a dog some company.

A food toy can calm an anxious dog.

You will need a tough rubber toy designed to be stuffed with food (see page 16 of Training Equipment). For the next five weeks your dog will receive its daily food intake only through the toy and in your absence. Divide the day's ration into five portions to stuff into the toy. If it ignores the food in the toy, simply place the whole thing in a plastic container back in the fridge until the next lesson.

If the dog eats the food willingly, it will have learned to do so in your absence and will associate your absence with a powerful food reward that takes time to extract. It is being rewarded for being separated from you.

If your dog barks or scratches to attract your attention, ignore it. Enter the dog's room only when it is silent. It must not come to associate its barking activities with your arrival. Remember—no tidbits or food at any other time!

Helpful Distractions

Some trainers recommend leaving a radio on while you're out to keep the dog company. This works in a few cases. Even more effective is the use of a tape recorder to play back the sound of your own voice to the dog while you are away.

Some dogs that bark when left alone can be distracted by leaving them food treats or a favorite toy to keep them busy until your return. You will need to prevent access to toys and chews when you're at home so that they become a special treat associated with your absence.

Excitable Barking for Attention

This type of barking can be a social nuisance when it gets excessive. The way to deal with it is by using counterconditioning. For example, if the dog barks when it sees you eating, stop feeding the dog by hand and give it food only in its bowl. Don't allow the dog any food reward if it stares or barks at you. Employ the ignore response. Better still, don't allow the dog in your presence when eating.

If your dog reacts with boisterous barking when you take the car keys or pick up its lead and collar or your coat, then simply confuse the dog's ability to anticipate your actions. This is done by altering walk times whenever possible, picking up the aforementioned articles 5 or 10 times a day, or even putting on your coat and walking to the front door only to return to your sofa. This saturates the dog with so many false starts not leading to the expected result that (unless it's really stupid) the message will get through.

Training disks, when properly introduced, are a very effective means of stopping this type of behavior in attention-seeking, dominant, boisterous dogs. While the dog is barking, throw the disks near the dog so that the sound startles it into silence. When your dog stops barking, don't make a fuss of it. Wait impassively for a minute of silence, then limit your praise to a softly spoken **"Good dog."**

Right: If your dog barks in anticipation when you put on your coat for a walk, confuse its expectations by making repeated false starts

Training Tips
- Don't reward bad behavior.
- Confuse the cues that elicit barking.
- Keep calm—shouting only adds to the excitement.
- Interrupt the barking by throwing training disks near the dog only at the time of barking.

12 • *Destructive Behavior*

Most destructive behavior—typically chewing objects like shoes or household furnishings—is caused by one of three factors:
• Normal puppy behavior. A puppy naturally investigates the exciting new world, often by chewing as much of it as possible.
• Boredom. When a dog is insufficiently active or stimulated as it grows from puppy to adult dog, it specifically targets certain items in the house to play with (in its view) or damage (our view).
• Separation anxiety. This is the most common reason. A dog that has not learned to spend time alone becomes stressed when separated from its family and may seek relief in frantic action, often causing drastic damage. This behavior may be accompanied by urination, defecation, barking, and whining. If you believe this is your dog's problem, see pages 54–59 for the way to tackle separation anxiety.

Prevention is the best remedy, and it's worth starting by looking at preventive measures.

Prevention Advice
(for puppies and newly acquired dogs)

It is important to have a dog who can be left unsupervised. So from an early age gradually accustom your dog to being left alone; aim to work up to periods of one hour. Don't encourage it to be under your feet all day. Instead, allow it to spend time by itself in the yard, on the patio, in a dog pen, or in another room while you're elsewhere. This encourages self-reliance and prevents a dog from becoming overly dependent upon its owner.

A new dog or puppy should never be allowed to roam the house freely for the first few months until you are able to judge its all-around behavior. Most chewing takes place in your absence. By curtailing your dog's freedom, you limit any damage to a single location, which is easier to deal with.

Below: *Dogs that do this to the cushions when you are out of the house are probably suffering from separation anxiety or boredom.*

Above: *As soon as you introduce a new puppy to the home, get it accustomed to spending time happily on its own inside its cage.*

Moreover, in the kitchen, for instance, you can implement preventive actions to teach the dog what it can and cannot chew. Eventually you can open up the house to the dog if that's your desire.

Exercise and Food

Exercising your dog before you leave it can help to burn off pent-up energy. It will be more likely to curl up and go to sleep than to rampage through the house. Tired dogs chew less! Consider feeding your dog before you leave the house (but make sure it's had ample time to evacuate its bowels before you go out). Satiated dogs become sleepy and lethargic and are less inclined to chew.

Cage Training

Puppies should become accustomed to an indoor cage from day one. Ensure that your dog sees the cage as a refuge rather than as a prison by providing marrow bones, toys stuffed with treats, or hide chews to keep it occupied inside the cage while you're out. When you return, make sure that you collect the chews and keep them locked away for next time you go out; otherwise your dog will not find them interesting. Feeding the dog in the cage once or twice daily also helps to condition it to accept it as a positive amenity.

If the destruction takes place in your absence, then it may be for the reasons mentioned above. Dogs that have not become gradually accustomed to your absence may become anxious when left. They must be taught that being alone is not the end of the world.

Destructive Behavior

Direct Action

Punishing destructive behavior can be difficult because we're often not at home when the destruction takes place. Punishment after the event is useless. If you come in and find your house trashed with the perpetrator peacefully asleep among the wreckage, feeling angry with it is only natural. It doesn't come naturally to the dog to link your immediate anger with something it did earlier. All punishment will achieve is to confuse it. All you can usefully do at this stage is to clean up and resolve to begin a retraining program immediately. However, if your dog is destructive in your presence or you catch it in the act, then there are a couple of measures you can use.

Have several ready-filled water pistols about the house. When you catch your dog chewing,

squirt water at its head, simultaneously commanding **"No."** (Alternatively, you can simply use the squirt without the command.) As the dog comes to associate chewing with an unpleasant squirt, it is less likely to enjoy this activity. However, this approach is effective with puppies and dogs in the early stages of destructive chewing only and will not affect dogs exhibiting anxiety-related destructive behavior.

A more direct means of training by association is to throw a bunch of training disks, keys, or a check chain near the dog's legs when you catch it chewing so that the noise distracts it and interrupts its actions. When using the water

Below: Admonish a dog for destructive behavior only if you catch it in the act. After the event is too late for direct action.

pistol or training disks, remember that all correction must take place at the time of the incident.

Do not physically hit the dog, take hold of it, or shout at it as this is not effective. In some cases it even encourages the dog to chew, for it may interpret this as a reward. After all, for some dogs attention of any kind is better than none.

Bitter Experience

If you have a dog that primarily chews specific objects, first try and use a deterrent spray. In this way, the dog learns from its own actions that chewing these things is an unpleasant experience that leads to a bitter taste in its mouth. Dogs don't repeat unpleasant experiences too often. Repetitive bitter experiences put the dog off chewing. The weakness in this procedure is often the owners. They forget to keep up the spraying or think that an occasional squirt is enough. It isn't—you need to fix in the dog's mind that these items always taste bad. Spray the objects when your dog is not in the room, and leave a window open for ten minutes before allowing the dog back in. This ensures that the dog can distinguish the spray scent on the objects to be avoided rather than sensing its presence throughout the room. Simultaneously, leave the dog a chew and interesting toys—the kind designed to be

Below: Remember to apply deterrent sprays on a regular basis. It is no good forgetting about the plan after only a day or so of remedial action.

stuffed with food that the dog can extract a bit at a time is ideal. This means that while the deterrent spray steers it away from forbidden objects, the dog has something that it is permissible and pleasant to chew.

If in severe cases your dog's behavior is resistant to discouragement, you may need to consider using an outside pen and kennel for a few months until the problem can be dealt with properly. Your dog will need to be gradually accustomed to using the pen, working up from five minutes two to three times daily. Remember to leave the dog some interesting toys filled with treats. Then when you're not at home you can know your dog is quite safe—and so is your home.

13 • Aggression—Dealing With An Emergency

Warning

Any dog that shows aggression should ideally be seen by a canine behavior practitioner, especially if children are present in the house.

The topic of how to deal with dogs that display aggression, either toward members of their own family, visitors, or strangers or toward other dogs is a huge and important one. Indeed,

Above: *Displays of aggression directed at people constitute a very serious problem for dog owners.*

displays of dominant aggression and fear-based aggression are the most common problems that I am asked to deal with professionally at my Canine Behaviour Centre. A detailed study of aggression is, however, beyond the scope of this book, which concentrates on obedience training and the elimination of problem behaviors around the house. Readers who are experiencing problems with dogs that display aggression are strongly advised to seek expert advice. They will also benefit from consulting *Breaking Bad Habits In Dogs*, a companion volume in which I devote a large section of the book to an in-depth consideration of the subject. In essence, you will be shown how to employ a technique like the Leadership Program to demote your dog psychologically and to boost your role as the pack leader in combination with a comprehensive regimen of obedience training.

What To Do if Your Dog Is Attacked in Public

What is appropriate here is some basic advice on what to do in an emergency if either you or your dog are attacked by another dog while out in public. A dog running wildly toward you might be friendly and have nothing more fearful in mind than saying hello, but its bulk and speed can be quite intimidating. In the worst case, you may be dealing with a fierce animal intent on terrorizing you and your dog. I've met people who have such a phobia of dogs that the prospect of walking across a park causes them misery. Though these are extreme cases, they're indicative of the fear that uncontrolled dogs can inspire. If you fear being on the receiving end of an attack by an aggressive dog, read on for advice on how to deal with the situation.

Dog-on-dog aggression can erupt very suddenly.

When dogs attack other animals, they normally go through a three-stage process:

Stage One: Predatory aggression, identify prey. Potential victims are sized up, and one is singled out.
Stage Two: Predatory aggression, pursuit. Suddenly they take off at full speed toward their target dog.
Stage Three: Predatory aggression, the kill. The final stage is the actual attack. That's the wolf ancestry in your dog revealing itself.

If you or your dog is attacked, here are some suggestions on how to deal with the situation and defuse the crisis.

Before you adopt any of the defense methods that follow, do try to be certain that the approaching dog has aggressive intentions before you act. Otherwise you could precipitate a fight when otherwise there would not have been one—your dog might be simply and correctly displaying appeasing

behavior. An example is when a very dominant dog approaches yours, and your dog appears frightened. You may feel that you need to rescue your dog from this humiliating or dangerous situation. By misreading and interfering, you can cause a fight. Sudden movement or shouting can activate the flight-or-fight mechanisms of the dogs. When they meet, dogs use a wonderful variety of body language signals that generally defuse tension and identify rank, sex, and age.

Aggression—Dealing With An Emergency

Passive Defense

If you or your dog are unlucky enough to be attacked in the park, this can be a very frightening experience, especially if your dog is small or timid and the attacker is large. In cases where the aggression is mostly vocal, simply telling your dog to sit and keeping your body between the two dogs will stop the situation from becoming worse. It is amazing how the aggressive dog will not come too close to a human to get at its canine target—circum-navigating an owner takes more courage than normal. (This will not work if your dog is also barking aggressively.) The antagonist might be expecting your dog to flee so the chase can begin. By keeping your dog calm, disappoint-ment will be its reward.

Below: If the threat from a dog appears to be mainly vocal, try to get your dog to sit calmly behind you. Don't risk your personal safety if there is a chance that the dog will bite.

Object Defense

If the dog is very aggressive and is attempting to bite or you believe from its body language that it will bite, then try holding a solid object like a stick or bag in front of your body with an outstretched hand. Don't be threatening or wave it. This display will normally distract the aggressor's attention and, if a bite does take place, the object is normally what is bitten. You need to appear calm and make few sudden movements while adopting these defensive actions.

Alternatively, you may have to let go of your dog if you feel that your own safety is in jeopardy. In the final analysis I can advise but not anticipate every possibility. It's your decision.

These actions are not, however, applicable to children when walking dogs. **They really must try and get help.** Children should carry a screech type alarm for summoning assistance.

Umbrella Rescue

The most successful method I have found to stop dog attacks on you or your dog is a telescopic umbrella. It's called defense enlarge or DE. This method is now standard defense advice at my behavior center. The basic idea is that most aggressive dogs are not as confident as they appear. By carrying a telescopic

1 *An umbrella can prove a surprisingly effective defensive aid if you are suddenly confronted by a dog with aggressive intentions.*

2 *Most dogs stop in their tracks and bark at the umbrella—only a few try to pursue the attack by getting around the edge of the shield.*

3 *If the dog moves left and right trying to get around the umbrella, simply roll it along the ground in the appropriate direction to maintain a shield.*

umbrella on your person, you are equipped with a superb quick-action device.

If you believe that a dog is about to attack your dog, then simply activate the umbrella release button as the tormentor approaches, also pointing it in the direction of the attacker. The sudden pop of the umbrella will take the dog by surprise. Keep your dog either on a lead adjacent to your body or hold it by one arm. During tests in more than 300 practical situations of aggressiveness, only two dogs did not either run off or just bark until their owners arrived and controlled them. The other two dogs snapped at the umbrella but never quite figured it out and did not pursue the attack further.

As the aggressor begins to bark, stand still and place the fully extended umbrella in front of you with its outer edge touching the ground. Then roll the umbrella clockwise or counter-clockwise according to which way the aggressor is circling you. The antagonist will find it difficult to bypass the defense.

The behavioral principle involved is based on the bluff principle familiar in the animal kingdom. We have all seen in television documentaries how some lizards expand the ruff around their necks when threatened by a predator to look larger than life. This trick works for them, and the good old umbrella can work for you and your pet dog in the same way.

14 • *The Training Program*

To help your dog reach a good basic standard of obedience I have set out a general training plan that is based on a 21-day schedule. All the training disciplines referred to here are described and illustrated in subsequent sections of the book. The lessons learned in week 1 are used and developed during weeks 2 and 3. However, don't make the mistake of thinking that the schedule is set in stone or that you cannot vary it as seems appropriate to your progress. It is simply there to give you a basic framework on which you can build. Try to apply the plan bearing in mind your dog's breed, age, and individual circumstances. If your dog is reasonably well behaved but just needs to learn basic dog training, then without doubt you should reach the desired standard in 21 days. For people who are training very young puppies the course is fine, but continuation training is essential. A little extra effort will be needed with older dogs that are more unruly and have perhaps been through other training courses, but you should still reach a good basic standard of obedience.

Training Timetable

Split each day into three lessons, and train for approximately 15 minutes per lesson. Puppies require only about five minutes training per lesson. If you wish to train four or five times daily, that's fine and will speed up training. If the dog still seems interested and keen at the lesson's end, you may train for a little longer but never to the point where the dog begins to become bored. Remember to play a fun game with your dog at the end of the lesson—this really does help to teach the dog to look forward to its training.

Week 1

Heelwork Walk (heel) in squares, and figure eights around trees, along roads, and in your yard.
Sit position 3 times per lesson.
Stand position 3 times per lesson.
Down position 3 times per lesson.
Stay on a lead 3 times per lesson.
Recall exercise 1–5 times in your yard and house.
Retrieve at lesson's end, and then enjoy a fun game.

Week 2

Heelwork Walk in the heel position—in and around the house, along the street, in the park.

At the heel, **Sit** position 5 times.

At the heel, **Stand** position 5 times.

At the heel, **Down** position 5 times.

Down/Stay Drop the lead and walk away; face your dog 3 times for a duration of up to two minutes.

Sit/Stay Drop the lead and walk away; face your dog 3 times for a duration of up to one minute.

Stand/Stay Drop the lead and walk away; face your dog 3 times for a duration of up to 30 seconds.

Recall exercise 5 times. Practice in yard and park (quiet area).

Week 3

Heelwork Walk in the heel position—in and around the house, along the street, in the park

At the heel **Sit** position 5 times.

At the heel **Stand** position 5 times.

At the heel **Down** position 5 times.

Down/Stay Drop the lead and walk away; face your dog 3 times for a duration of up to three minutes.

Sit/Stay Drop the lead and walk away; face your dog 3 times for a duration of up to two minutes.

Stand/Stay Drop the lead and walk away; face your dog 3 times for a duration of up to one minute.

Recall as many times as practicable. Practice in yard and park (quiet area).

Advice Before You Start

Begin your training in a garden, yard, a peaceful part of the house, or another place with no distractions. Continue to practice there for the first lessons until you have reached a standard whereby the dog responds to your commands. If the dog is progressing well, you can then ask family members to distract the dog mildly, which will allow you to reinforce your commands and maintain the dog's focus on training despite what's going on around it.

Once your dog understands the basics of each command, the next stage is to practice all of the exercises in different training locations, the street, park, or other public places. Note:

when near a road or on a sidewalk, all exercises must be carried out on a lead—**no exceptions**.

At first the dog will be distracted; this is normal, but now you have to work harder. The dog may find the distractions more interesting than you or what you are trying to teach it. This is a time when a number of owners give up, because their dog appears to be regressing, but this is not the case! The dog does not forget what you have taught it but instantly comes to expect either your enforcement of the obedience, or lack of it, in these situations. The dog has to be obedient in all circumstances, so do not give up—keep going! Within a few days, the dog will respond to your commands.

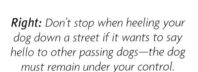

Below: Finish a training session with some play and a retrieve game so that your dog associates training with fun.

Right: Don't stop when heeling your dog down a street if it wants to say hello to other passing dogs—the dog must remain under your control.

Training Tips

1 Before you begin training your dog, be sure you fully understand the exercise you are about to teach. Do not attempt any exercise if you are in doubt. If this is the case, refer to the book again.

2 The motivation for your dog to learn is praise (and other rewards) delivered in a pleasant tone of voice. Remember this throughout the training program. Few dogs need frequent physical correction—rely on patience and repetitive training with a play period at the end.

3 If your dog is having a bad day, try standing still and think about your actions and the way you are training; at least that stops your dog from getting its own way. You can be sure that if the dog appears to be making errors, the fault lies with the trainer not communicating the message clearly enough to the animal. It is not necessarily a matter of deliberate disobedience.

4 When training, the dog may begin to lose interest. If that's the case, get it to do an exercise it likes, praise it, finish training, play a short game, and then begin again later in the day.

5 When teaching the recall on a long line in a public place, do not allow your dog to play with other dogs, as the line may get tangled in their feet. If too many dogs arrive, call your dog to you, praise it, and then put the dog on its normal lead and walk off.

Left: Be aware that different breeds, born with different working instincts, progress in training at different rates.

15 • Heelwork

Dogs that pull are a nuisance—especially if the dog is large and strong. Being dragged along can be a serious problem and certainly it is an unpleasant experience. Dogs that drag owners usually don't get walked as often as dogs that are obedient and are a pleasure to walk. Only certain members of the family are strong enough to control the dog, so this has a detrimental effect on the lifestyle of many dogs. Of course, even the worst doggy pullers in the world are not trying to upset you personally. They are completely unaware of your plight. By far the majority of dogs I see for problem behavior like excessive pulling have already attended a dog-training course and this has been unhelpful for a number of reasons. The training program I use is effective, however, and it starts teaching you about canine communication.

I use certain basic commands for simplicity and consistency—you may use your own commands if that suits you—but they must be short, preferably just a single syllable. Praise should be given in a very soft tone of voice so that the dog can distinguish commands from praise. Equally, the dog should understand the word **"No,"** and this should be delivered in a sharp, commanding, crisp tone. Deliver your command **"Heel,"** then walk off. If the dog remains by your side, whisper **"Clever"** or **"Good dog."** If, after a few strides, it begins to wander ahead, command **"Heel"** firmly, tap your side simultaneously, and, if the dog returns, give soft verbal praise.

For control, make sure you have the correct lead and collar. I always teach my dogs to walk on my left and at my heel. In my view it helps if a dog knows consistently which side it's walked on. All dogs do not have to walk in this exact position, but this does make for continuity and enables you to use your hands to assist in training. You may wonder why we position the dog on our left but usually hold the lead in our right hand. This is because it leaves the left hand nearest the dog as a working tool. The right hand controls the lead. The best position then is to have the dog at your left side with its head about level with your body. This is known as the heel. It enables you to turn in any direction without tripping over the dog.

Left: This dog is walking nicely at its owner's left side with its head more or less in line with her body. The lead is held in the right hand.

Right: *Walking a dog that consistently pulls is no fun. When you are dealing with an animal as big as this, it is exhausting and potentially dangerous. If you own a dog, it really is vital that you should train the dog to walk obediently at your heel.*

Begin your heelwork training in a garden, backyard, quiet part of the house, or any other place where you will not be bothered by distractions. Continue to practice there for the first few weeks until you have reached a standard whereby the dog responds consistently to your heel and sit commands.

Right: *If your children participate in the training program, make sure that you are all consistent. This girl should ideally have the dog on her left.*

Beginning Heel Training

Let's now focus our attention on adult dogs and the basics of heelwork that they must learn. (Information about training puppies can be found later in the chapter on pages 106–109.) The main purpose of teaching a dog to walk comfortably by your side is to enable the two of you to negotiate sidewalks and streets and to weave your way through crowds of pedestrians who do not necessarily take any notice of your dog and its position.

Therefore your dog should learn to stick close by your left side so that wherever you walk it will be nearby. To help teach the dog this work, we use a number of bodily techniques known collectively as the heelwork turns. In simple terms, we employ visual, verbal, and physical communication to make our intentions clear to the dog. We use our arms, legs, and body movements to nudge, guide and maneuver the dog to respond to our directions and to stop it

1 *For heelwork, I recommend that the dog should be positioned on your left side and the lead held in your right hand.*

2 *When you are ready to begin training, deliver your **"Heel"** command in a firm tone of voice, tap your thigh with your left hand, and walk off to the front.*

3 *Initially the dog may well surge ahead of you. If that's the case, command **"Heel"** again, and when the dog returns to your side, praise it in a gentle tone.*

pulling on the lead ahead or tripping us up by moving across our path.

The dog must learn to keep an eye on its handler—you. We are talking teamwork. When we walk along chatting to a friend, we instinctively keep close as we move through hordes of other pedestrians. That skill probably took us years to learn since childhood, and we have a concept of what we are doing and what we want to do. The dog has no such notion and is being asked

to learn this technique in a very short period of time relative to its human counterparts.

Heel: Walking Forward

Begin with your dog sitting on your left side. Your right hand holds the lead with a slight loop across to the dog's collar. If your lead is 6-feet (2 m) long, then loop it once to shorten it. Your left hand comes into play only if the dog begins to surge ahead—otherwise it's free. This may seem odd at first to the beginner. When ready, walk off tapping your side with your left hand and command **"Heel."** If the dog surges or begins to get ahead of you, command **"Heel"** again, tap your left thigh, and praise the dog when it returns to your side.

4 *Use your free left hand to tap your side to let the dog know where you want it to position itself as you repeat the command* **"Heel."**

5 *Praise your dog at the end of the exercise—make a fuss over it and tell it that it's a* **"Clever dog."**

The Lead Check

If your dog will not return to your side when you command it, it may need an attention-gathering check on the lead. Take the lead in both hands and check the lead sharply once, releasing it immediately. Do not drag the dog back. This check is more of a complaint/interruption. It lasts about a tenth of a second. As the dog is momentarily halted by the check, command **"Heel"** again and encourage the dog in an excited tone to return to your side. Use lots of praise and touch rewards upon its return. If the dog really pulls hard ahead, stop momentarily, command **"Sit,"** pause, and begin again. Don't forget that the turn techniques described next also teach the dog not to surge ahead. When all the turns are combined on a walk, the dog learns that it must pay attention if it is to see where you are walking because it is unable to predict your sudden changes of direction. For the dog not to be caught unaware, it has to be positioned at your heel to see you all the time.

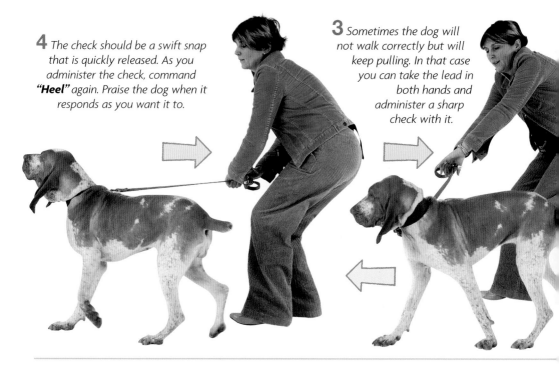

4 *The check should be a swift snap that is quickly released. As you administer the check, command* **"Heel"** *again. Praise the dog when it responds as you want it to.*

3 *Sometimes the dog will not walk correctly but will keep pulling. In that case you can take the lead in both hands and administer a sharp check with it.*

1 To begin heelwork training, have the dog positioned on your left, walk, tap your left side, and command **"Heel."**

2 If the dog starts to pull ahead or you sense that it is about to do that, command **"Heel"** again, and tap your side to reestablish control.

5 Make sure that the dog gets plenty of praise, pats, and perhaps a tidbit when it has trained well. Rewards help to cement the progress you have made.

81

The Left Turn (puppy safe)

Walk in a straight line and then turn left across the dog's front. Pivot on your left foot, and use your right knee to emphasize the turn left. Your right hand naturally holds the lead, and simultaneously while making the turn, your left hand joins it so both hands are together for control. Pull the lead into your waist. When you have turned left, your right hand collects any slack lead and your left hand is now free to use for petting, touching, or tapping your side for encouragement as the dog stays close

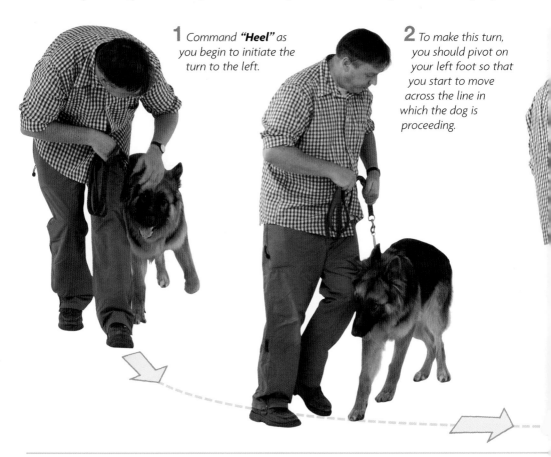

1 *Command **"Heel"** as you begin to initiate the turn to the left.*

2 *To make this turn, you should pivot on your left foot so that you start to move across the line in which the dog is proceeding.*

by your side. Dogs that don't pay attention often get a surprise at this sharp left turn and quickly learn to pay attention to what you are doing, rather than what they are interested in, like scents. A bit of amateur dramatics also helps—act excited and use quick movements. This behavior combined with an animated tone of voice encourage a reticent dog to turn quickly and walk or trot toward you as you head off in the new direction. It's also fun.

3 *As you pivot on your left leg, raise your right knee high in an exaggerated manner and use it to direct the dog's head toward your new direction of travel.*

4 *Once the dog is moving in the desired direction, you can use your free left hand to give it a brief pat or to tap your knee to encourage it to keep close to your heel. Praise it with a gentle* ***"Good dog."***

The Left About Turn (puppy safe)

This begins like the left turn described on the previous pages but instead of turning left at a 90° angle, you actually pivot fully back through 180° so that you are facing in the opposite direction. Command **"Heel"** as you begin the turn. This takes a little practice. Once mastered it really does help to teach your dog not to pull and to pay attention to you. It is quite a dramatic full turn. As you walk off again in a straight line, give lots of dramatic praise for the dog being back at your side. With larger dogs your right knee may nudge/guide the dog to a semihalt as you turn back on it before you walk off in the opposite direction. Keep your commands snappy—a listless trainer will have a listless dog for company.

Right: *When seen from behind, this view of the about turn shows how the swiveling movement that you make on your left foot takes you back in the direction from which you came.*

1 *For the left about turn, you spin fully around and head in the opposite direction.*

2 *Command **"Heel"** as you begin the turn. As you make the pivoting movement, the dog will come to a semihalt for a moment.*

Making Turns with a Smaller Dog

When practicing turns with medium and large-sized dogs, you will find that you can use your knee to emphasize the movement you are making in order to help coax the dog into altering direction with you. With smaller dogs this is not possible as they carry their heads too close to the ground for the handler's knee to come into play.

When training with small dogs, you have to rely more on your own body language, leg tapping, and excited verbal praise to keep the dog moving in parallel with you. With smaller dogs, you may also use your right foot to nudge the dog to a semihalt as you pivot. Try to maintain the dog's interest by acting in an animated way.

2 *Instead use verbal praise and taps of your leg to help keep the dog alert to your commands and direction of travel.*

1 *Small dogs cannot be guided by the handler's knee in the way that larger dogs can.*

The Right Turn (puppy safe)

Walk in a straight line and turn sharply right, pivoting on your left foot and striding out with your right leg. You lower your body, and again your left hand joins your right on the lead. This time you drop your hands low to give the dog more lead length as you turn right. Remember it will be surging straight ahead unaware at first of your turn to the right. If the dog sees your turn and begins to turn also, praise it enthusiastically as it returns to your left side. Once you are upright again and

walking straight, let go of the lead with your left hand. Remember to keep the lead loose but not too long otherwise you cannot quickly control the dog if it surges ahead again. Dogs that pay attention are not often surprised by this sharp right turn and learn to be watchful of your movements. If you use an excited tone of praise to encourage your dog back to your left side, this really helps the dog to concentrate on you. Once walking normally, stop talking and praise the dog occasionally for still being by your side.

4 *Praise your dog with a softly spoken "**Good dog**" as it follows you obediently around the turn.*

3 *Bend lower as you swing around and drop your hands to give the dog a bit more lead length through the turn.*

1 *Take up the slack if using a long lead, and command **"Heel"** as you walk forward. This German Shepherd Dog is looking alert in anticipation of whatever may happen next.*

2 *To make a right turn, you pivot on your left foot. This may catch the dog by surprise as you are turning away from its direction of travel, so reinforce the movement with a **"Heel"** command.*

The Right About Turn (puppy safe)

The right about turn also begins like the right turn, but you make a full 180° turn back along the route that you have just walked. In other words, if the dog is not paying attention it will now be walking in one direction, while you are walking in the opposite one. However, the lead connects you both and soon makes your intentions clear. As you execute the turn, command **"Heel"** to give the dog the opportunity to turn with you and to receive your praise. Remember to give dramatic praise if the dog begins to turn and return to your side.

Once you have mastered all the turns, preferably in your yard or house first, the dog will quickly start to appreciate the fun of training and be happy to concentrate on your actions. You are now leading. The dog is led but also enjoys learning to walk on a loose lead by your left side.

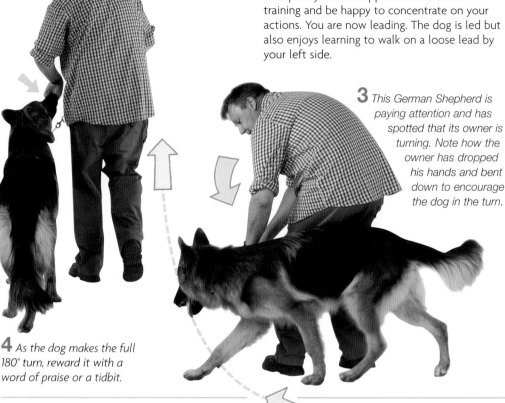

3 *This German Shepherd is paying attention and has spotted that its owner is turning. Note how the owner has dropped his hands and bent down to encourage the dog in the turn.*

4 *As the dog makes the full 180° turn, reward it with a word of praise or a tidbit.*

1 *When making a right about turn, you will be turning away from the direction in which the dog is walking. Keep the lead length reasonably short so that you remain connected.*

2 *For the about turn to the right, you pivot sharply on one leg and walk off in the opposite direction. Command* **"Heel"** *as you execute the turn.*

Training Tips

• With all the turns command **"Heel"** as you turn; this alerts the dog that you are about to change direction.

• Praise the dog, telling it that it is **"Clever"** in a whisper if it keeps by your side during the turn. Use food or a toy as an added attraction.

• If you need to check the dog, make it a short, sharp snap on the lead and more of an inconvenience to the dog surging ahead. Don't drag the dog to you at any time.

• If you are using food as a reward, make sure it's in your left pocket or in a hip bag so that it's easily accessible to give as you make a turn.

• Always use touch to gain your dog's attention, and always use verbal praise when it performs obediently.

• If your dog is food orientated, use a choice of succulent tidbits; if it is play orientated, use a squeaky toy to encourage it to follow you around a turn.

House-Training Plan

Strange as it may seem, begin lead training in the house. Most dogs react excitedly when the lead is produced, so let's use that conditioned enthusiasm for indoor training. Clip the lead onto the collar but simply walk around the home. If your dog likes treats, use bits of cheese or ham as rewards. Your dog is on your left and the lead is in your right hand. The treats will be administered by the left hand, so perhaps wear a coat with baggy pockets for easy access to the treats in the left pocket. Command **"Heel"** and walk off. When you turn left, right, left about, or right about, command **"Heel."** If your dog stays near your side, offer a treat. If it surges ahead, about turn and simultaneously bend low and hold the treat near the dog's nose. Draw the dog into you as it follows the treat back to your left side. Give the treat, say **"Heel,"** and praise with a **"Clever dog."** Be dramatic! Over-the-top performances attract dogs more than monotonous training styles. Of course, with highly strung dogs that get overexcited, tone down the drama.

1 *You can practice lead and heelwork training by walking around your house and making turns with the dog at your side.*

4 *When doing circuits like this, vary your left and right turns to stop the exercise from becoming monotonous.*

3 *Praise the dog and tell it that it's* **"Clever"** *if it stays obediently at your side.*

2 *Command* **"Heel"** *each time you make a turn, and perhaps offer a treat.*

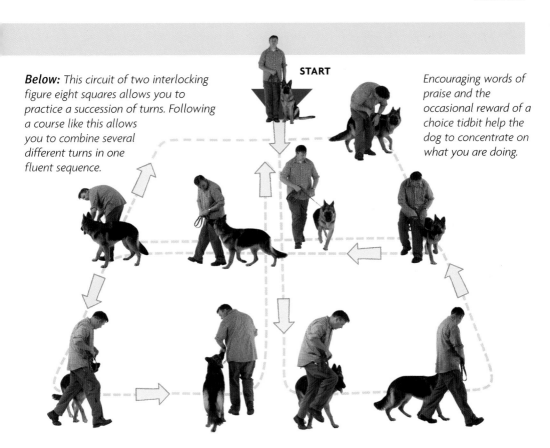

START

Below: *This circuit of two interlocking figure eight squares allows you to practice a succession of turns. Following a course like this allows you to combine several different turns in one fluent sequence.*

Encouraging words of praise and the occasional reward of a choice tidbit help the dog to concentrate on what you are doing.

Backyard Training Plan (puppy safe)

If you have a yard, perform the same routines outside but now include a figure eight or interlocking square pattern into the heelwork. Your main concern is to make sure that the dog's attention is focused on you. Remember to keep tapping your left side, and offer a few excited words of encouragement as the dog nears the proper heel position. A positive response from you occurs only when the dog is approaching or is at your side.

In larger rooms or bigger yards, if the dog seems to be losing interest or wishes to pull toward an enticing smell, then break into a trot or run. This ignites many dogs' interest, as movement for dogs is intrinsically exciting. Run for a few yards or so and then drop back to a walk again once the dog has come by your side.

Heelwork With Dogs

The next stage in your heelwork training is to practice the heel exercises in different training locations as well as on the sidewalk, in the park, and in other public places. At first your dog will be distracted; this is normal, but now you have to work harder. The dog may find the distractions more interesting than you or what you are trying to teach it. This is a time when a number of owners give up, because their dog may appear to be regressing, but this is not the case!

When heeling your dog down a street, it is natural, when other dogs pass by, for your dog to display curiosity toward them. Don't stop—just carry on walking, praising your dog as it comes back to your side. Maybe at this point offer a treat as a greater distraction

than the passing dog. Equally, you can snap check the lead on an adult dog if it stubbornly pulls toward them. Don't use the snap check, though, with a puppy.

Sometimes I begin to run for few yards, and most dogs find this exciting and prefer to follow rather than pull toward the other dog. Your dog must not come to think that every time it sees another dog in the street or park it no longer has to listen to you. Obviously, you do wish your dog

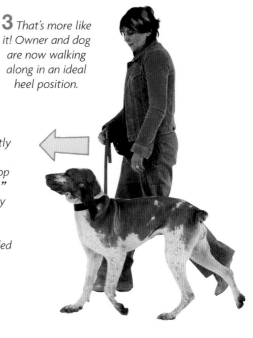

3 *That's more like it! Owner and dog are now walking along in an ideal heel position.*

Left: If your dog persistently pulls ahead of you when walking down a street, stop and command it to "Sit." Start walking again only when it has calmed down. Repeat this as many times as needed to get the dog to obey the "Heel" command.

to play and socialize with other dogs at times. This is perfectly acceptable, as long as your dog is under control. If you believe, however, that by stopping and allowing your dog to exchange sniffs with the passing dog, this will satisfy it and reduce the problem, you are mistaken. It will just teach your dog that a new dog approaching means we stop.

I use another technique with adult dogs. If the dog really surges ahead, I stop, tell the dog **"Sit,"** and do not move again until it calms down. I have stopped a hundred times with one dog on a long stretch of road until that particular Labrador got the message that if you pull, I stop. Patience is obviously required, and you may need to persist over many weeks of training. If your dog lags behind you, under no circumstances pull it; just use praise to encourage it back to your side.

2 *Instead, you should pat your side and use words of praise—* ***"Good dog"****—to encourage it to catch up with you.*

1 *If your dog lags behind you when practicing heelwork, do resist the temptation of hauling it physically back to your side by tugging on the lead.*

Street Heelwork

Just walking from your house to the park or through town is another important part of teaching a dog new rules of obedience. With dogs that tend to pull off to the left a good deal or dogs that at first don't concentrate, I will walk next to walls and fences quite closely to prevent any lateral straying. This means that the dog can now pull only forward or backward. If it pulls forward, I will about turn, commanding **"Heel"** while offering a treat or squeaking the favored toy to gain the dog's attention. Many dogs soon catch on to changing direction quickly with you, lured by the reward and the vocal praise as they near your left side again.

For dogs that ignore these rewards—and many dogs do—I snap the lead for just a fraction of a second. This is not meant to pull the dog back, so be careful not to do this. It simply sends a pulse of energy down the lead to the dog's neck and serves as a way of gathering its attention. When the dog feels the snap, it generally looks in your direction. At this point you command **"Heel"** and tap your side while bending low. As the dog starts to align itself with you again, indulge in a little bit of amateur dramatics so the dog thinks that this is really fun. You must turn every time the dog surges. Repetition begins to teach the dog where you, the leader, want it to be in relation to your person.

3 *The squeak of the toy is the reward that lures your dog around as you change direction. Praise the dog if it stays close by your left side.*

2 *A sharp squeak with the toy should be enough to regain the dog's attention. The handler here has the lead in her left hand as she feels more comfortable with the toy in her right.*

1 *One method of dealing with a dog that surges or pulls off to the left is to use a favorite toy as a lure to encourage it to stay close by your side.*

Heelwork Tips

• Change your daily route as often as possible. Dogs that cannot predict routine are less likely to pull.

• If your dog is particularly bad on any occasion, stop and tell the dog to **"Sit."** If necessary do this near a fence or railing *(left)* over which you can drop the end loop of the lead. At least you can have a breather and collect your thoughts, and your dog will be impressed with your firmness not to move.

• Constantly executing right or left about turns when walking along pavements, and adding frequent sit positions, teaches the dog that a walk involves a set of rules that, when obeyed, bring rewards, not conflict.

• If a dog becomes bored while you are training in the yard or park, take out a favorite toy and throw the toy for the dog to retrieve. Dogs learn to associate the play time with the heelwork training.

Heeling A Dog To A Car

1 *The dog should be walking calmly to heel as you approach the car— don't allow mad scrambling to get in.*

2 *Tell your dog to "Sit" at a little distance from the car. If it obeys, you may open the door.*

Most dogs love cars but can become over-excited when they approach one. This section explains what to do if you have problems getting your dog into the car because it is too excited. Before leaving the house, make sure the car door is closed but not locked so that it is easy to open. Approach the car and then suddenly about turn and walk back to the house. Sometimes vary the door that you use and open the rear or side door. As the dog expects to leap in, command **"Heel"** and tap your left side. Walk away and repeat this three or four times or until the dog calms down. Practice this many times over the course of a week or so, until a sense of order has been reestablished.

If possible, park you car next to a post, fence, or railing over which you can drop the lead and that allows the dog to get close to the door but not actually into the car. As the lead tightens as the dog strains against the post, command **"Sit."** Wait about a minute. Praise the dog if it sits quietly, but ignore the dog if it gets excited. Begin to take the lead again only if the dog is calm. After many repetitions and over many days, the dog will start to realize "I don't get in the car by pulling." Remember always to tell the dog to sit a short distance from the car. You may sometimes walk away from the car taking the dog with you to eliminate its sense of expectancy. Only after the dog has sat and you have said **"In"** does the dog get in the car.

3 *If the dog sits quietly, command **"In."** Shut the door if it tries to enter too soon.*

4 *The dog gets in on your command—that's the new discipline. Every now and then call your dog out again and repeat the procedure.*

Sometimes you should even call the dog back out of the car several times so that it can never predict the routine. The dog in time will become calm and learn this series of commands and actions: **"Sit"**—place lead on—**"Heel"**—walk to front door—you go through the door first—dog is called through with **"Heel"**—walk to car without pulling—**"Sit"**—dog sits on command by the car door—door is opened—dog is told **"In"**—dog gets in.

Right: *You can deal with a dog that becomes over-excited as you approach a car by confusing its normal expectations. Just as it seems that you will open the car door, about turn, command **"Heel,"** and walk away. Repeat this a few times—the dog will calm down as it will not know when the car door will really be opened.*

At The Park—Letting The Dog Out

For overexcited dogs, especially large strong ones, place the dog's lead over a hook or handle inside the car so that when you open the door, the dog cannot physically jump out. Tell the dog to **"Sit."** Wait with the door open and then gently unhook the lead. When ready call the dog out with **"Come."** As the dog leaves, command **"Sit."** As the dog's front feet hit the ground, shorten the lead immediately so that you have more control pulling the lead upward but not tightening it. Use your sit training techniques to complete the sit. Now position your dog by your left

side with **"Heel"** and make it sit again. When you are ready, off you go to the exercise area. It is not recommended that you disconnect the dog's lead as soon as you enter a field, park, or recreational area. Walk at least a hundred yards into the park, and then tell the dog **"Sit."** Wait a minute or so, and then release the dog with **"Free."** Most people with difficult dogs let them go immediately because of their bad behavior, but this just teaches the dog that it is released when it wants to be, rather than on your command.

1 *When it is time to let your dog out of the car again, open the car door and instruct the dog to* **"Sit."**

2 *If it stays calm, pick up (or unhook) the lead and command the dog to* **"Come."**

Walking with a Stroller

The first rule is to walk with the dog on your left. Initially, push an empty stroller along the street for a few hundred yards while the dog gets used to the noise and appearance of this unfamiliar object. Command **"Heel"** in the normal way. Observe your dog's reactions, and encourage it with praise and a few tidbits if it seems a little fearful. Most dogs quickly adapt. Place your child in the stroller and walk the dog with it only when the dog walks perfectly alongside. Never wrap the lead around your hand or the handlebars—if the dog panics or becomes scared, the consequences could be awful.

3 *Make your dog **"Sit"** as soon as it is out of the car. Move off when you choose to and when the dog is ready to walk calmly by your side to the park or exercise area. Make the dog sit again when inside the park before letting it off the lead to play.*

Stopping Dogs Pulling

There is no doubt that dogs that pull on the lead are the bane of many owners' lives. Next to not coming when called, heel training of dogs that pull is the most common problem presented to a dog trainer or behavior practitioner. If you find that your dog does not respond to your heelwork training when working with a normal collar and lead, you may need to use different equipment, such as a face collar or body harness. They are simple to use and effective in stopping dogs from pulling. In the following pages I explain how to fit and use them. **Note:** face collars and body harnesses should be used only on determined adult dogs—**do not use them on puppies or sensitive dogs**.

Below: *Dogs that pull on a lead are exhausting to handle. One remedy for such behavior is the use of a face collar or body harness.*

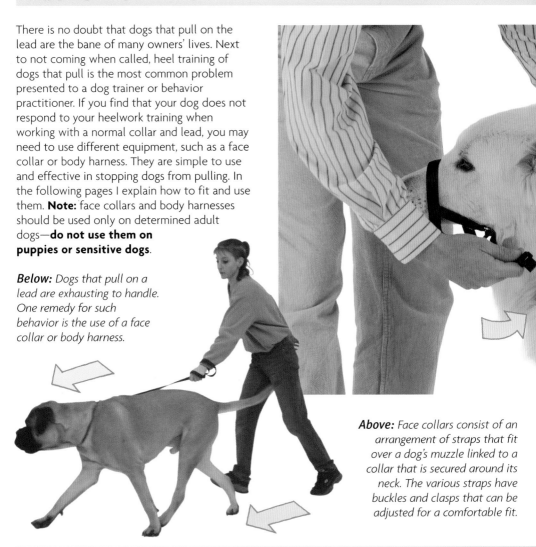

Above: *Face collars consist of an arrangement of straps that fit over a dog's muzzle linked to a collar that is secured around its neck. The various straps have buckles and clasps that can be adjusted for a comfortable fit.*

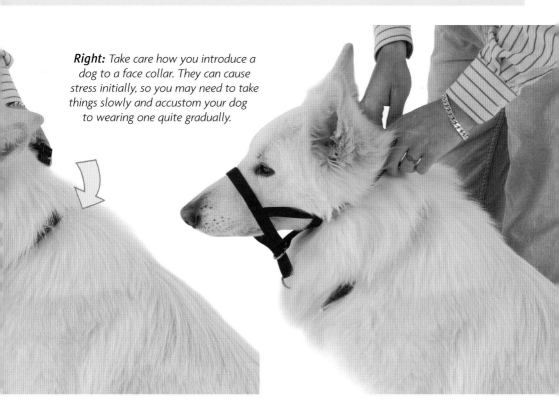

Right: *Take care how you introduce a dog to a face collar. They can cause stress initially, so you may need to take things slowly and accustom your dog to wearing one quite gradually.*

Using Face Collars

A face collar fits over the dog's muzzle. It allows the dog's mouth to open as usual so that it can breathe normally. When the dog pulls ahead of its owner, the face collar checks the dog's head back toward the owner, making pulling uncomfortable or awkward for the dog. They do work well on most, but not all, dogs,

I have found that determined or difficult dogs do settle down and learn not to pull. One drawback is that they can sometimes rub on the dog's face, causing some minor abrasion of the skin surface. However, if fitted properly they are without doubt an efficient way to stop a determined puller from stretching your arms.

How To Introduce A Face Collar

It is very important to introduce the face collar to your dog slowly and to build good associations with it in your dog's mind. Most people rush the introduction and then become upset at their dog's stressed reaction to it. You can avoid some of this by following this advice.

First, get your dog to sit wearing a conventional collar. Have several juicy tidbits at hand. Then place the face collar on your dog and reward it with a tidbit. Leave the face collar on your dog for a few minutes; give it a food reward intermittently. Your dog should now associate having the face collar fitted with receiving a reward. This needs to be repeated three times daily for about ten minutes each over a period of three days. Next, attach the lead to the face collar and walk your dog a short distance around the house or yard; reward your dog at short intervals. If your dog panics or attempts to rub its head on the floor (which is normal), distract it with the food and use your lead to help it sit. Alternatively, the dog can wear the face collar around the home for 15 minutes three or four times a day to get accustomed to it.

Most dogs resent the face collar at first but quickly adapt to it and come to associate it with food rewards and walks. Once you can walk your dog around the house or yard without adverse reaction, you're ready for normal outdoor use. Do persevere and don't give up or feel sorry for your dog. Otherwise you'll be back to square one.

Have a supply of juicy tidbits at hand with which to reward your dog when you first fit the face collar.

3 *When a dog has come to accept wearing a face collar without a fuss, you are ready to attach a lead and to begin to walk it around the house and yard in the heel position. The next step is then to venture into the outside world and continue training in other locations.*

1 Once you have fitted the face collar, reward your dog with a tidbit. The dog will now associate wearing the face collar with a pleasant experience.

Left: Once a dog has become accustomed to being walked around the house and yard while wearing a face collar, you are ready to venture out into the wide world. The action of the collar should prevent the dog from pulling against your control.

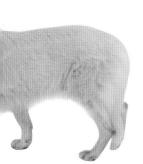

2 For the first three days, simply leave the face collar on the dog for 15 minutes at a time so that it becomes accustomed to wearing one. The odd tidbit given as a reward from time to time will also help to sugar the pill.

Body Harnesses And High Check Collars

Antipulling Harnesses

Harnesses are available to help stop dogs pulling. They are not to be confused with a general dog harness that helps dogs to pull more effectively. A typical antipulling harness has thin cords that pass under the dog's front legs (armpits) so that when the dog surges ahead, the cords pull tight on the dog's armpits, causing physical discomfort. When the dog stops pulling, the discomfort disappears. The dog dictates its own comfort level, and in this way many dogs quickly stop pulling.

The High Check Collar

This training technique should be applied only to dogs that are very difficult to train to heel. It is only appropriate with medium to large dogs. It is called the high check because a fixed or slip collar is placed high on the dog's neck just below the ears. The slip collar is made of thick, smooth nylon and is designed to tighten on the dog's neck if it pulls. It is kept high in this position throughout the walk because it prevents the dog from using its neck fully as a pulling lever. It also stops the dog lowering its head into a low driving position in order to use its body power and neck muscles to pull you forward and so force its way ahead.

You operate the high check more or less like a normal lead and fixed collar. Instead of having a loose lead between the collar ring and the lead clip, the distance between your hand holding the lead and the high check collar attached to the dog is only about 12 inches (30 cm)—the lead is kept very short, but not excessively taut (it has a little slack in it). If the lead is left too loose, the high check collar will slip lower down on the dog's

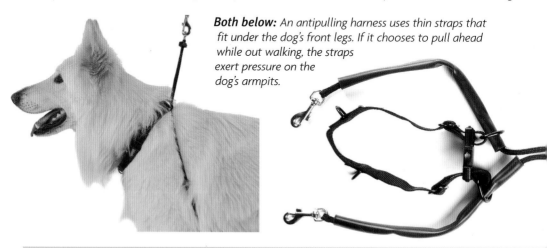

Both below: *An antipulling harness uses thin straps that fit under the dog's front legs. If it chooses to pull ahead while out walking, the straps exert pressure on the dog's armpits.*

neck into the normal position of a collar and so become ineffective.

When the dog attempts to surge ahead, it is simply not able to use its body power. At the same time, the collar becomes uncomfortable on its neck when it pulls. The dog discovers that life is uncomfortable if it pulls but comfortable when it does not pull. I find that once a dog has learned not to pull on a walk, you can allow the slip collar to fall back into a normal collar position or even preferably switch back to a conventional fixed collar.

One word of warning: **don't use the high check on puppies or toy breeds.** It is not suitable for small dogs.

Above: *The underleg straps pass through buckles on the collar, down under the front legs and then back up to the collar, where they are clipped in place.*

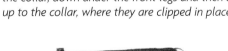

Right: *A high check collar sits further up the dog's neck than usual. It inhibits the dog's ability to lower its head and drive forward.*

Heel Training For Puppies

When one trains a puppy on a lead and collar, it's obvious that these little creatures are incredibly malleable and can learn to walk next to you in a matter of weeks providing there is enough motivation in your handling. This chapter is mostly concerned with dogs that pull. However, giving some basic training information for puppies is useful here because that's the ideal time to train a dog. I train from six weeks of age. Other people may think that's too young for training, but I disagree. In my professional capacity, I have only seen positive results when training from this age. I begin training in the house, hallway, kitchen, and yard. Each session lasts just a few minutes.

A puppy has no idea what you want or why walking on a lead and collar somehow involves not pulling. Why should it? There is no place in wolf evolution for a collar and lead nor walking at our pedestrian pace, which is slower than the

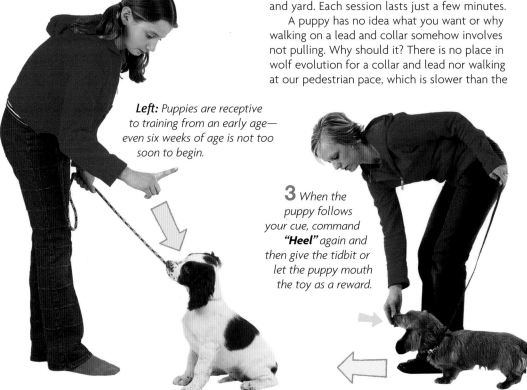

Left: Puppies are receptive to training from an early age— even six weeks of age is not too soon to begin.

3 *When the puppy follows your cue, command* **"Heel"** *again and then give the tidbit or let the puppy mouth the toy as a reward.*

1 *When heel training a puppy, use a food tidbit or a squeaky toy to give the puppy a tangible reward.*

dog's natural gait. However, once a puppy has been habituated to the collar and lead in the home, we can begin heelwork tentatively. Puppies do not require checking.

I always use a cue link when dog training. This means that I motivate the dog by some action that gives me its attention and then give it a corresponding reward when it acts correctly. This gives the puppy pleasure. Using a tidbit and/or a squeaky toy, I walk off giving the command **"Heel."**

2 *Command **"Heel"** and walk off with the puppy on your left-hand side.*

Training Recap

• With puppies and less-determined adult dogs, practice heel training using rewards to reinforce good behavior.

• You can start training a puppy to walk to heel on a lead from six weeks of age. It pays dividends to train during this formative period of its development.

• **Don't** use face collars, body harnesses, or a high check collar when training puppies. They should be used only on strong, determined adult dogs.

Puppy Training On And Off The Lead

When the puppy surges ahead of me, I turn to the right, simultaneously bending down with an outstretched left hand that is either holding a squeaky toy or proffering a tasty treat (very tiny). As the puppy takes a cue and follows my hand, I command **"Heel"** and give the tidbit or let the puppy mouth the toy. After repeating this action ten or more times, I throw the toy for the puppy to make a little game and finish. I begin a new lesson later. The puppy has now begun to pay attention, to learn the command

"Heel," and has found that being by my side at all times brings fun and rewards.

Puppies will often panic when they are first connected to a lead and collar, so it imperative that you allow the puppy to get used to the lead and collar before any training begins. You can do this by simply allowing the pup to drag the lead about while in your company. You can also hold the lead and reward the pup with some tidbits. If at any stage the puppy lunges ahead and begins to panic when the lead

5 *Finish with praise and perhaps a little game. Keep a sense of fun when training young dogs.*

"What a smart puppy!"

4 *As the puppy takes the cue, command **"Heel"** again to link the verbal signal to the action. Then give the puppy the tidbit or let it mouth the toy so that it feels rewarded for what it has just done. Repeat this exercise nine or ten more times to cement the lesson.*

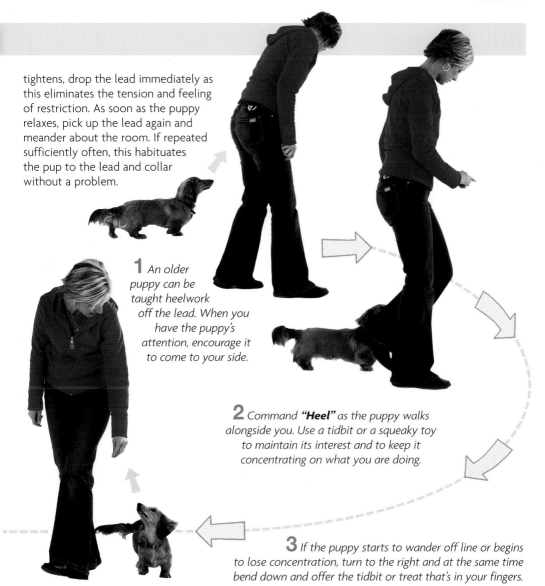

tightens, drop the lead immediately as this eliminates the tension and feeling of restriction. As soon as the puppy relaxes, pick up the lead again and meander about the room. If repeated sufficiently often, this habituates the pup to the lead and collar without a problem.

1 *An older puppy can be taught heelwork off the lead. When you have the puppy's attention, encourage it to come to your side.*

2 *Command **"Heel"** as the puppy walks alongside you. Use a tidbit or a squeaky toy to maintain its interest and to keep it concentrating on what you are doing.*

3 *If the puppy starts to wander off line or begins to lose concentration, turn to the right and at the same time bend down and offer the tidbit or treat that's in your fingers.*

16 • *Stay Positions*

Teaching dogs to sit, stand, and lie down on command are excellent exercises that will be useful throughout the dog's life. A trained dog knows what is and what is not allowed and tends to be more relaxed, content, and controllable in our complex and demanding society. Untrained dogs, like badly behaved children, are not welcome in many places. So begin training these three exercises in the knowledge that your dog's education is developing fast.

Initially the sit, stand, and down will be taught so that the dog clearly understands which position relates to which command.

Then, we will complete the lessons with the stay exercise in all three positions, which of course broadens the dog's overall obedience plan.

This training should be part of the three 15-minute daily lessons that form the backbone of your training regimen. Initially these can be organized about the home and yard, while the third lesson of the day can take place before or during a walk. Some owners who have unmanageable dogs outside the home may wish to do all of their training in the home for the first week until they have instilled some basic obedience—that's fine as long as the dog gets plenty of exercise through games after each training session.

If your dog has very ingrained bad habits—maybe it is a rescue dog or has not had adequate formal training—the problems may be embedded. For instance, you may own a dog that has pulled on the lead for a very long time while being walked. The learned behavior will be embedded and the pulling will be a part of the dog's natural routine that it has practiced many hundreds of times. In a perverse way, this is also dog training—but training of the wrong kind. Now our new training programs should be able to fix that.

Below: Aim to make teaching the stay positions part of your daily training program.

Left: Note how the dog is alert to the verbal ***"Stay"*** command and the corresponding hand signal.

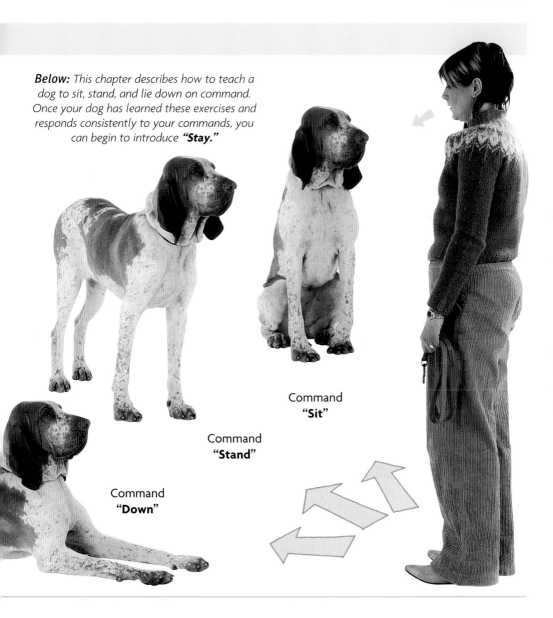

Below: This chapter describes how to teach a dog to sit, stand, and lie down on command. Once your dog has learned these exercises and responds consistently to your commands, you can begin to introduce **"Stay."**

Command
"Sit"

Command
"Stand"

Command
"Down"

Teaching The Sit Position (puppy safe)

Teaching your dog to sit is without doubt one of the easiest lessons to accomplish, and most people have little trouble with it. Dogs are lower to the ground than us, and they tend to look upward at our faces. This articulation of their body helps us to encourage the sit. A lead and collar can be used, but most dogs learn the sit just as well without one.

*Left: Food is a very potent aid in teaching puppies to sit. Hold a food bowl or tidbit above your puppy's face and issue the command **"Sit"** as it naturally drops into a sit position. Then reward the pup.*

Puppies learn to sit quickly, and a choice tidbit or the sight of its food bowl across the kitchen creates great excitement as we assume the bitch's roles as surrogate mother. We can hold the food bowl or tidbit just above the pup's face, and two things will happen beside some vocalization of excitement. The pup will naturally sit, and simultaneously we should deliver a crisp command **"Sit."** Then offer the reward we have in hand. Days later, the pup should be sitting even before the command is given thanks to repetition, reward, and maybe its observance of your body language. So why don't dogs just sit when told to, and why do so many people have difficulty getting a reliable sit out of a puppy or adult dog?

Let's examine the situation when we taught the dog. We were in a quiet training location like the kitchen. We used a powerful reward. A clear command was followed by praise and the food reward. When the dog is in other rooms, the yard, or a park, the greatest challenge to you as the trainer is to obtain the sit position considering the amazing variety of distractions that vie for the dog's attention. Here I am going to enter the dog's mind with you and explain several methods that will enable you to teach your dog to sit, stand, and lie down on command.

Sit Using Food (puppy safe)

Food is a powerful means to attract a dog's attention and is my first port of call as a trainer. Start in a quiet room and

1 *Attract your dog's attention with a food treat. As the dog approaches, bend down and offer the treat just in front of and above its nose.*

hold the tidbit just above the dog's nose. When it walks forward eagerly to get the treat, command **"Sit"** and slightly pass the hand holding the treat up and over the dog's head so that it actually needs to look upward to keep its eye on the treat. Most dogs will naturally fall into the sit position. As they do so,

2 *Then pass your hand up above the dog's head and command* **"Sit."** *As it looks up to follow the treat, it should drop into a sit position.*

immediately give the treat. So we have **"Sit"** and then a treat delivered virtually within a second or two.

Repeat the exercise several times during each of your three lessons a day and at feeding times. Using your feeding routine will help cement the **"Sit"** training.

Sit Using Toys *(puppy safe)*

Most dog owners buy dog-friendly toys, particularly squeaky ones. If your dog is toy orientated (most are if they are introduced to them early enough), then select the dog's favorite toy and use the toy like the food tidbit described on the previous page. Position yourself in the same way, holding the toy aloft. When the dog sits, immediately throw the toy. The chase is the reward for the dog entering the sit position on command. Have a thin, light lead attached to the dog so that you are able to recover the toy from an eager dog wishing to play chase with its new trophy. If you have already taught the retrieve, then the lead is not needed. Remember, as with all toy training, keep the toys locked away from the dog at all other times during the entire training course. Doing so helps to keep the dog enthusiastic.

1 *A favorite toy can be used in much the same way as a food tidbit to teach the sit. Squeak the toy to attract the dog's attention and call it to* **"Come."**

2 *As the dog runs toward you in anticipation of a fun game of chase and retrieve, raise the toy up and over its head so that it naturally starts to look upward.*

Get On Down
If working with smaller breeds or puppies, you may need to be in a crouching position or even kneeling on the floor to help encourage the dog's body into the natural sit position with a food treat or favorite toy.

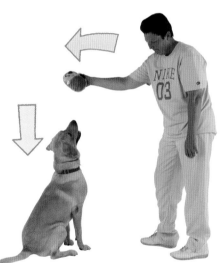

3 *The dog's eyes will follow the toy and it will drop back into a sit position. Command* ***"Sit"*** *as the dog's haunches settle on the ground. Then reward it with praise.*

4 *Then command* ***"Fetch"*** *and quickly throw the toy for the dog to chase. Play is another potent reward for sitting obediently when commanded to do so.*

Ignore And Sit (puppy safe)

This approach truly shows dog training psychology in action. It does require patience on your behalf. When applied consistently, it trains a dog to sit in a more natural and less direct manner. So when you first enter a room where the dog is and it comes over to say "hello," just command **"Sit"** and look directly at the dog while holding your empty hand upward though with no treat. The dog is now learning signals and commands simultaneously.

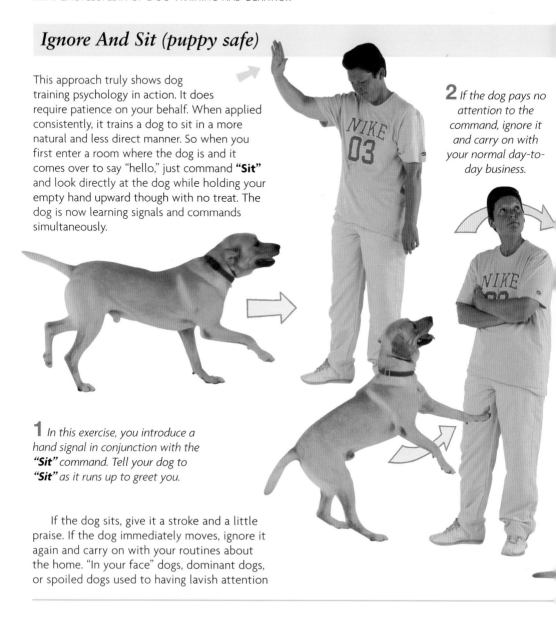

2 *If the dog pays no attention to the command, ignore it and carry on with your normal day-to-day business.*

1 *In this exercise, you introduce a hand signal in conjunction with the **"Sit"** command. Tell your dog to **"Sit"** as it runs up to greet you.*

If the dog sits, give it a stroke and a little praise. If the dog immediately moves, ignore it again and carry on with your routines about the home. "In your face" dogs, dominant dogs, or spoiled dogs used to having lavish attention tend to need a lot of interaction. After about ten minutes when you can see the dog out of the corner of your eye, again call it to you with a **"Come"** command. As it arrives, command **"Sit"** again. If it becomes too excited to pay attention to you or just stares at you with that big doggy grin, walk off again and ignore it. The dog will not expect this. I find that they quickly catch on that you now decide when attention is given and praise will come only when they assume the sit position on command.

3 *A few minutes later, call the dog to you and command "Sit" again. If that's a failure, ignore it again and repeat the exercise until you do achieve success.*

4 *The dog will eventually learn that the praise and attention that it craves so much will be given only when it assumes the sit position on command.*

Sit Using A Hook

For very boisterous or very large breeds of dog that jump up a good deal and are hard to control because of their exuberant behavior, we need to use some short-term extra equipment. These dogs are often animals that have just not learned that you don't like their aberrant behavior, however well meant it is.

Fix hooks securely in several locations about the house—into baseboards or screwed to walls. In the yard you can use outdoor furniture like fence posts or a secure wall. These are

useful when trying to teach an excited dog the sit. Take the dog's lead—this generally arouses great interest—and attach the lead to the dog. Make sure you are next to a hook fixture. Hold the food or toy and command **"Sit"**—simultaneously drop the lead over the hook so that you have your hands free (except for the treat). As the dog feels constrained, you can step back and then forward again, completely in charge of the situation. When the dog assumes the sit, give it the food treats. This method

4 *When your dog is sitting nicely, give it the treat. The hook allows you to keep control of the situation. Finish by giving the dog some words of praise and a few pats and strokes.*

3 *By rocking forward while you give the command* **"Sit"** *and coaxing the dog with the tidbit, you will be able to encourage it to fall into a sit.*

stops the dog from climbing all over you and reduces the need for you to handle the dog, which in most cases is the reaction the dog has learned to obtain—the reward of body touch and a fun game. Through repetition around the yard and the house, the dog soon learns that by sitting calmly it receives a treat. Using different locations teaches the dog that this command can take place anywhere around the home.

2 *You now have your hands free and can stand just out of the dog's range in quiet control of the situation. Command **"Sit."***

1 *When training very lively dogs, to use a hook that will restrain the dog and allow you to control its movements. Begin by dropping the end of the lead over a conveniently situated hook.*

Quiet Moments

It is important with all the exercises to command, then reward, and to allow quiet pauses in between so that the exercise is not a continuous ramble of words that only makes learning more difficult for the dog.

Sit: Forward And Back (puppy safe)

This style of training is again quite subtle and relates to your deportment and body language. It works on all types of dog but is especially good for dogs that are sensitive or deferential and dogs that tend to get panicky if you over-handle them. It can be used in conjunction with some of the other methods described. Simply call your dog to you in a room and, as the dog approaches you, run a few steps backward. This should encourage your dog to run forward to you—as it does so, take a step toward the dog and slightly lean over it. The sudden change of direction by the leader causes the dog to adopt a deferential position as it has to look vertically up into your face. If the command **"Sit"** is given during this action, the dog will normally sit. If that happens, praise it lavishly and walk off. Repeat several times.

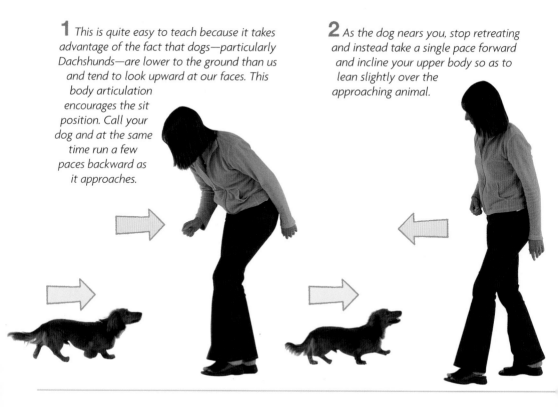

1 *This is quite easy to teach because it takes advantage of the fact that dogs—particularly Dachshunds—are lower to the ground than us and tend to look upward at our faces. This body articulation encourages the sit position. Call your dog and at the same time run a few paces backward as it approaches.*

2 *As the dog nears you, stop retreating and instead take a single pace forward and incline your upper body so as to lean slightly over the approaching animal.*

Take Time to Praise and Reward

As usual, finish the exercise with words of praise and plenty of pats and strokes. If you have established the proper hierarchy of the family pack, your dog will view the approval of its pack leader as a very powerful reward.

3 *While leaning forward, command "**Sit**" and at the same time use the sit hand signal to reinforce the verbal command. The dog should fall back into a sit position.*

4 *Dogs are very responsive to visual signals and human body language, so it pays to back up verbal commands with a consistent set of visual cues like this hand signal.*

The signal for sit ends with the arm and hand extending upward like this.

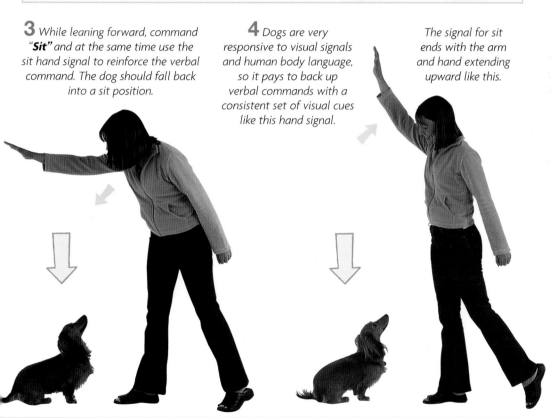

Sit: Lead And Collar Style (puppy safe)

1 *Practicing the sit exercise presupposes that your dog will play along and remain attentive to you. Of course, some dogs are not like this—they have their minds on other things and tend to run off. This is where the use of a lead allows you to keep control.*

Let the lead hang loose so that the dog feels comfortable with it.

Using the lead and collar is again useful with dogs that tend to run off or are difficult to control. Hold the lead in one hand and have some food treats available in a fanny pack or a suitable pocket. You use the technique described in the Sit Using Food (page 112). Hold the tidbit just above the dog's nose. When it walks forward eagerly to get the treat, command **"Sit"** and slightly pass the hand holding the treat up and over the dog's head so that it actually needs to look upward to keep its eye on the treat. Most dogs will naturally fall into the sit position. As they do so, immediately give the treat. So we have **"Sit"** and then a treat delivered within a second or two.

Once the dog has the general idea of the sit—which on average takes about 30 sit practices over a few days—and you are confident enough to progress, we can begin to teach the sit/stay position. We are now adding a link to the sit and we will do the same later on for the next two positions: the stand and the down.

2 Call your dog toward you for a treat, and as it approaches command **"Sit"** and move your hand up and over the dog's head.

3 The dog will look up and naturally drop into a sit position. If it does this, deliver the treat immediately. The sit and the reward are thus linked in its mind.

4 Finish, as always, by offering generous praise. You are happy—the dog has behaved; the dog is happy—it's getting stroked and fussed over.

123

Sit/Stay—Introducing Hand Signals

Tell the dog **"Sit"** and, placing the flat of your hand in front of the dog as an additional signal, command **"Stay."** Move no more than one step away from the dog's side. Wait about three seconds and say **"Stay"** once more, then move back to the dog's side. Praise the dog immediately using voice and touch. It is not necessary to proffer food every time, but perhaps every third or fourth time as you practice the lesson. Always

allow some slack in the lead so that it never tugs on the dog's neck, as most dogs will move toward you if this occurs, however mild the tug. If the dog becomes too excited when you praise it or offer a treat, use only verbal praise and at a level that will not excite the dog and encourage it to move.

The important part of the training exercises relating to the stay position is the time that

The flat of the hand signals that the dog should stay.

1 *Once your dog remains in the sit position consistently, you are ready to introduce the "Stay" command.*

2 *To begin with, move only about a pace or so away from your dog. You are really trying to cement the time that the dog will remain sitting.*

3 *Turn and face your dog while reinforcing the "Stay" command verbally and with a hand signal. After a few seconds, step back.*

the dog is left in that position, not the distance that you move away from the dog. Strange as it may seem, most people seem to want to walk a fair distance from the dog rather than wait for a period nearby. Time and solidity are required as a first stage in this sit/stay lesson. If you can reach the end of your lead by training lesson three on day one, you are doing well.

3–5 seconds: First lessons
30 seconds: By the end of week 1
1 minute: By the end of week 2
2 minutes: By the end of week 3

4 *Now praise the dog. Gradually build up the time that you ask your dog to remain in the sit/stay over the 21-day course.*

When To Drop the Lead
You should not attempt to drop the lead until your dog comfortably accepts you walking away from it to the limit of the lead and then walking back after a few seconds without it moving. It must wait for your praise or the occasional tidbit.

After your dog will happily remain in a sit for a few seconds when you walk away to the full length of the lead, you are ready to drop the lead and extend the distance a little.

125

Stay And Circle On The Lead

2 *Give a firm **"Stay"** command, use the hand signal to reinforce the order, and step off from the start position.*

1 *Once your dog is solid in the basic sit/stay, you can think about extending the distance you walk and returning in a circular path.*

3 *Walk out to the full length of the lead and then turn and face the dog who ought to be still sitting patiently in the sit position.*

Many dogs that remain steady at a distance of a yard seem to lose the stay when you decide to walk back to the dog in an a counter-clockwise circle. Their little heads spin trying to keep you in sight and suddenly their rump moves from the sitting position. The best way to remedy this is to command **"Stay"** sharply just as you are about to walk around your dog counterclockwise. Continue to walk around the dog and return to the dog on its right-hand side. When the exercise is complete, you and the dog should be facing the same way with it on your left still sitting obediently.

Many people when returning to a dog that is in the stay position hesitate on their return to the dog if it begins to move or looks as if it will do so. In fact, unwittingly, they thereby take much longer to return than otherwise would be the case, which makes the stay a longer exercise in duration than it should be. This is unhelpful in these early learning stages. Always move quite quickly, not hesitatingly. If you seem indecisive, the dog may waver.

Sit/Stay Recap

So now let's recap on the sit/stay actions in order.

- Dog and handler stand beside one another as if about to heel off. Tell the dog to sit and stay.
- Walk to the end of the lead feeding it out as you do so. If the dog does not move, face the dog for a second or two, and then immediately return using the same route.
- Give the dog one more command as you return to emphasize that you want it to stay.
- Walk around the back of the dog in a counterclockwise direction. Then quickly bend down and praise the dog. The lesson is complete.
- For variety, repeat this in different locations in the house and yard.

5 *When you pass behind the dog and out of its view, the dog's concentration may start to waver. Don't dawdle at this stage.*

6 *You should end up where you started with the dog sitting quietly on your left.*

4 *Command **"Stay"** again. After a few seconds, begin to walk back to the dog. Give another **"Stay"** command as you start to walk around the back of the dog.*

Sit/Stay—Time and Distance Training

Once your dog is staying reliably at a distance of a yard or so, increase the time span of the exercise to about two minutes but still at the same short distance—this is critical to future training stability. You can do this by increments of about 30 seconds per day. Do not try and increase the time too quickly as this may ruin the continuing positive training and the rewards that the dog associates with staying in the sit position. Dogs learn quicker if they are rewarded continually for doing it right rather than if their training is intermittently interrupted for correction because we are trying to run before we can walk.

Once the dog is staying each and every time for at least a minute, you are making good progress. Often in training you will find that a dog

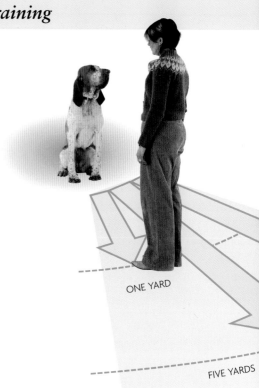

ONE YARD

FIVE YARDS

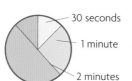

30 seconds

1 minute

2 minutes

Left: Gradually increase the duration of the sit/stays to around two minutes over the course of the three-week training program. Don't rush this, however. Fairly small increments of 20–30 seconds at a time are fine.

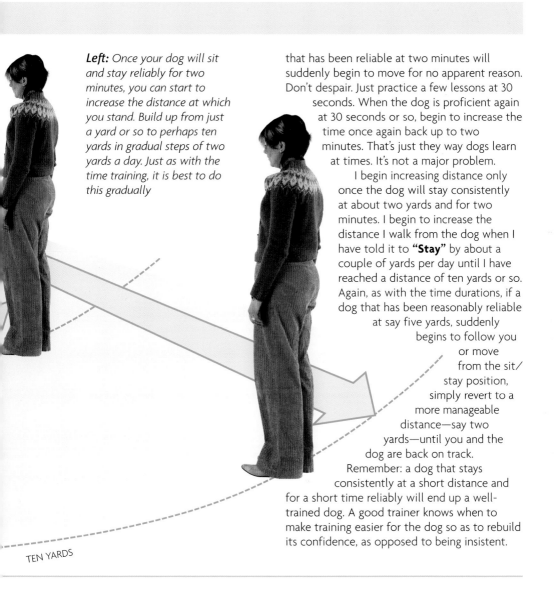

Left: *Once your dog will sit and stay reliably for two minutes, you can start to increase the distance at which you stand. Build up from just a yard or so to perhaps ten yards in gradual steps of two yards a day. Just as with the time training, it is best to do this gradually*

that has been reliable at two minutes will suddenly begin to move for no apparent reason. Don't despair. Just practice a few lessons at 30 seconds. When the dog is proficient again at 30 seconds or so, begin to increase the time once again back up to two minutes. That's just they way dogs learn at times. It's not a major problem.

I begin increasing distance only once the dog will stay consistently at about two yards and for two minutes. I begin to increase the distance I walk from the dog when I have told it to **"Stay"** by about a couple of yards per day until I have reached a distance of ten yards or so. Again, as with the time durations, if a dog that has been reasonably reliable at say five yards, suddenly begins to follow you or move from the sit/ stay position, simply revert to a more manageable distance—say two yards—until you and the dog are back on track.

Remember: a dog that stays consistently at a short distance and for a short time reliably will end up a well-trained dog. A good trainer knows when to make training easier for the dog so as to rebuild its confidence, as opposed to being insistent.

TEN YARDS

129

The Stand Position

This position is most useful for dogs; it helps with grooming, veterinary inspection, and when halting at a roadside. It is useful to command the dog to stand at the curb, especially on sloppy, rainy days when the sit position would cause the dog's rump to get dirty.

The stand position is also useful when going through doorways or if you need to stop and go while negotiating pedestrian traffic or similar obstacles. Show dogs are always taught to stand, as this is the glamour position exhibitors use for dog shows. The stand is also a position where your command should be crisp but not too loud. Any indication of verbal

Left: *It is useful to teach a dog the stand position—it has many practical benefits, as, for instance, when your dog needs to be examined by the veterinarian.*

1 *For this basic stand exercise, equip yourself with some choice tidbits and then call your dog to* **"Come"** *to you.*

2 *As the dog walks toward you, turn away to the right—in effect you are swiveling away from the dog and coming to a halt.*

correction will often send a dog into a sit or a down to escape what they assume will be their leader's overt sternness—even when none is intended. So take stand training more gently. Also don't let the dog linger in the stand position for more than a few seconds in the first training lessons.

3 *The dog will normally move to your left side to maintain eye contact. As it comes alongside you, command* **"Stand"** *and offer the tidbit just in front of its nose.*

Stand Using Turn and Food (puppy safe)

Most dogs learn the stand quite quickly. Less confident or low-ranking dogs often prefer to sit or lie down in case you—the pack leader—admonish them for standing too tall for their pack position. If this is the case with your dog, then be succinct but gentle. Definitely do not use force or the dog will immediately try and get even lower to avoid your displeasure.

No lead is required. This exercise is more informal and can be practiced anywhere in the house or yard. Call the dog to you. If your dog is an excitable type, keep the command firm and don't overexcite. As the dog walks to your front, turn to your right and stop. The dog will generally try to walk around you to keep eye contact. As it moves to your left side, command **"Stand"** and offer the food tidbit level with its nose or slightly lower. Let your dog take the food in this stationary stand position. Praise the dog also. Then walk off again a few steps. If your dog walks alongside you, repeat the stand exercise as described. If it doesn't follow you, call the dog to you, turn right as its nears you, and repeat the sequence of command, food reward, and verbal praise.

4 *Let the dog have the food tidbit while it is in the stand position, and praise it. Then relax, wander off, and repeat the exercise.*

Stand Using Collar And Lead (puppy safe)

The training method described on the previous page can be repeated using a collar and lead for more control. We can simply walk about the house in the heel position and then stop, simultaneously commanding **"Stand"** and immediately offering the treat as before.

Do not delay the reward with the stand otherwise many dogs will automatically sit, as that is how they have received treats in the other lessons. New commands are just new sounds to them and have no meaning until the link with a physical position is established.

1 *The method of teaching the stand with a turn and food reward that was illustrated on the previous page can also be used with a collar and lead.*

2 *While walking with you dog on the lead, stop, command **"Stand,"** and offer the treat just in front of the dog's nose. Then move off and repeat. Don't delay when giving the dog the tidbit, or it may easily drop into a sit.*

Stand Using Toys (puppy safe)

Whether you use a collar and lead for this exercise is optional—it really depends on how calm or excitable your dog is. A toy can be useful for teaching the stand position. The appearance of the toy excites the dog. Once you have shown the toy just out of reach of the dog's jaws, tell it **"Stand."** Wait a few seconds, and then throw the toy as a reward. Once you have the toy back, repeat the lesson. You should also lengthen the duration of the stand lesson over many repetitions. Within a week you should have your dog standing for a maximum of say ten seconds at this early stage before throwing the toy again.

2 *Show the dog the toy and then hold it in front of its head while commanding* **"Stand."** *Keep your dog in the stand position for a few seconds.*

3 *Then let the dog chase and retrieve the toy as a reward for obeying the stand training. Take the toy back from its mouth and repeat the lesson.*

1 *You can also use a favorite toy to teach a dog to adopt a stand position. The collar and lead is optional in this case, but they do give you an added element of control that can be useful with excitable dogs.*

Stand And Touch Tickle (puppy safe)

This is my favorite method and without doubt is a very successful way of teaching the stand. I use the collar and lead to walk the dog in the heel position around the yard or house. I halt and gently command **"Stand."** At the same time I place my left hand just under the dog's belly. There is a definite touch but not a grab. Most dogs seem to freeze when you do this much as they do when dogs sniff each other's underside. I am taking advantage of this natural reaction to touch this area. As soon as the dog freezes or just before it turns to see what you are up to, I quickly move my left hand to tickle the dog's back just above its tail for a second.

So I command **"Stand,"** take one extra step forward after the command to allow the dog time to stop, touch its underside, tickle its back, and praise all within a few seconds. Speed is essential. I then briskly command **"Heel"** and walk off again only to repeat the exercise several more times. Because different dogs are sensitive in different ways, you may need to adjust the touch and tickle method accordingly. We do not want the dog to become over-excited. This method certainly helps prevent dogs sitting all the time, which is often a problem encountered by people trying to teach the stand.

3 *Now swiftly tickle the dog's back near the top of its tail. This stabilizes the dog in the stand position. Praise it, and then repeat the exercise.*

2 *As the dog comes to a halt, quickly touch its underside. This usually causes the dog to freeze in the stationary position.*

1 *To train using the stand and touch tickle method, begin by walking your dog to heel. Then halt and command the dog* **"Stand."**

Stand Position—Problem Solving

My dog keeps sitting

You may be overpowering the dog. Don't overpower or tower over sensitive, low-ranking dogs as it makes them assume a lower position, thus slowing down the training. Dogs naturally learn the sit quicker than the stand. When teaching the stand, practice three stands for every sit initially until the stand is more stable.

My dog lies down

Use a lead and collar. Every time the dog attempts to lie down, tap your side and say **"Heel"** excitedly and move off swiftly for about two yards. As the dog nears your side, repeat the **"Stand"** command. Don't ever drag the dog upward with the lead, this ruins the stand training.

2 *Heel your dog for a few yards to get it active and responsive again, and then repeat the **"Stand"** command.*

1 *If your dog persists in lying down while you are trying to teach the stand, tap your thigh and command it briskly to **"Heel."***

Stand Using A Hook

As with the sit position, we can use a lead, collar, and hook fixed to a wall to teach the stand. This approach is especially useful for dogs that get overexcited or take time to calm down when food is produced. With smaller breeds you will need to adopt a lower posture in the early stages of training so as not to dominate or tower over a little dog.

Place the dog on the lead and attach it to the hook. Approach the dog with the food tidbit and, as the dog walks a step or two toward you, command **"Stand"** as it comes to a halt at the end of the now taut lead. Give a food reward immediately. Turn and walk away a few feet waiting for the dog to relax into the down or sit position. When it does so, walk

2 *As the dog approaches you, command* ***"Stand."*** *The lead will limit its ability to move.*

1 *A hook is a useful aid when teaching excitable dogs the stand. Drop the lead over the hook and approach the dog holding a tidbit.*

3 *When the dog is standing stationary, give it the treat as a reward. Turn away, allow the dog to sit or lie down again, and then repeat the exercise.*

back to the dog again and repeat the procedure once more. Three or four repetitions are normally enough. Once the idea has settled in and the dog seems to understand you—probably after the first week—you may return to the other stand training styles

An outstretched arm signifies **"Stand."**

Stand/Stay

The stand/stay while you actually leave the dog has some use on occasion. Once the dog stands consistently for at least 20 seconds next to your side or in front of you, simply follow the same format as described in the sit/stay routines except that the dog is in the stand position. Remember, don't make the dog stand for more than 30 seconds if you walk off as it is not the most comfortable position over a long period of time. There is no need to train a dog to stand for more than one minute.

Left: *Once a dog will stand consistently for you, move away a little and practice a stand/stay at a distance. Keep the exercises quite short—10 seconds is fine to start with and 30 seconds a suggested maximum. Finish off your training with a game that will allow the dog to burn off some of its excess energy. Stand/stays do not come naturally to many dogs, so you must reward a good performance.*

10 seconds

20 seconds

30 seconds

The Down Position

The down position is in my view the most useful training a dog can learn. It has many uses—you may be chatting for some time in the street with a friend or perhaps you are lining up for service and the dog needs to lie down to be out of the way. It also helps to teach the dog to lie in the corner of a room or on its bed when guests arrive. It is certainly a comfortable position for a dog to be in and a helpful aid.

The down/stay position can also help to control and calm excitable dogs. Once a dog has learned the rewards connected with **"Down,"** they love performing it.

Right: Dogs that will lie obediently in the down position—particularly when distractions are around, such as other animals or guests arriving—are a genuine pleasure to be with. Ensure that practicing the down is part of your family's obedience training regime.

Down Using Food (puppy safe)

In the house and yard get the dog into the sit position as it is easiest to train a dog to lie down from the sit. When the dog is sitting, extend a small treat like a piece of ham or cheese toward its nose with your right hand. As the dog stretches forward to take the food, drop your right hand down to the floor, enticing the dog's nose to follow suit. This naturally encourages the dog to slide downward into the down—as the dog lies down obediently, give it the tidbit while simultaneously commanding **"Down"** in a crisp tone of voice. Then verbally praise **"Good dog"**—remember that praise should be given in a soft whisper. Many owners forget to change their tone and the dogs hear only an indecipherable monotone throughout the lesson, which slows the training process. Repeat several times.

*Small girl, big dog—no problem. It knows that **"Down"** means down.*

1 *While your dog is sitting, use a small tidbit of food to attract its attention.*

2 *As the dog stretches its muzzle forward to take the offered treat, command **"Down,"** just draw your hand back a little, and encourage it to follow the tidbit down to the floor.*

4 *Now for some praise. Make a fuss over the dog—it's done well!*

3 *The downward motion in conjunction with the stretch toward the tidbit should cause the dog to slide into the down position.*

*Give your dog the treat and reiterate the command **"Down."***

Down Using A Toy (puppy safe)

You can achieve the same results as described on the previous page by using a toy instead of a food tidbit. Add variety to see what will work best for you and your dog. Begin by selecting a toy with which your dog really enjoys playing. Show the dog the toy so that you gain its attention, and then use the toy like the tidbit as an enticement to lure the dog into the down position. Once the toy has been placed on the floor and the dog has slid down to meet it, hold the toy in place for a few seconds and then throw it for a retrieve. Alternatively command your dog to **"Sit"** first, then, placing the toy near its nose, command **"Down"** and lower the toy to the ground. The dog should slide into the down and you should praise it enthusiastically. Pause—heel forward a few feet, and then repeat the exercise again.

1 *Most dogs have a favorite toy, and we can use this characteristic to teach the down by using the toy as a lure to encourage the behavior we want.*

2 *Place your dog in a* **"Sit"** *position and then gain its undivided attention by showing it the toy.*

3 *Command **"Down,"** and use the toy in the same way that the tidbit is used to entice the dog into a down position.*

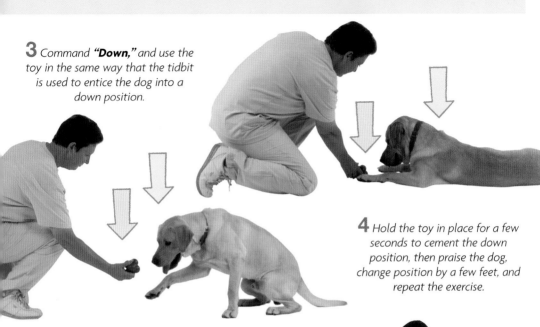

4 *Hold the toy in place for a few seconds to cement the down position, then praise the dog, change position by a few feet, and repeat the exercise.*

Play Power

Don't forget to conclude this training exercise by throwing the toy for a few retrieves. Your dog will welcome this as a release from the discipline of remaining in the chosen stay position. The dog needs to stay focused on the toy. The toy's power as an object of play is reinforced if it is used for fun and games at the same time as it is a training aid.

Right: *When the lesson's finished, make time for some fun so the toy remains a favorite plaything.*

Down Using A Collar And Lead *(puppy safe)*

Some handlers find using a collar and lead is more practical for all the exercises in the home or that their dog is much calmer when on a lead. That's fine—we simply repeat the food or toy method only the dog is now leashed. When the dog is lying down, may place your foot on the lead about 12 inches (30 cm) from the dog's neck. Remember that the lead must be loose and should not tighten

1 *For extra control, particularly when training large dogs around the house, it's a good idea to use a collar and lead. Show your dog the food tidbit in your hand.*

2 *Draw the dog into a down position by lowering the tidbit to the floor. As the dog sinks down in response to the food lure, give the* **"Down"** *command.*

3 *While the dog is in the down position, put your foot on the lead about 12 inches (30 cm) from its neck. Make sure that the section of lead between the collar and your foot is loose so that dog is quite comfortable. If it tries to sit up now, the lead will tighten and prevent it from getting up.*

when you place your foot on it. If it does, lift your foot for a second and let the dog get more comfortable; when the lead is loose, place your foot on it again. If the dog now decides to sit up, the lead will inhibit the upward action while simultaneously you will command **"Down."** This works with many dogs to prevent their upward movement. Do not drag the dog down. If the dog's rear end rises as it's about to get up, press down on the rump quickly before the dog has risen. Otherwise begin again. Don't get involved in a physical trial of strength as this will disorientate the dog and cause some panic. Remember to use the lead cautiously.

4 *When using your foot to secure the lead on the ground, do make sure that the lead is not growing taut and pulling on the dog's collar. Praise the dog for being a **"Good dog."***

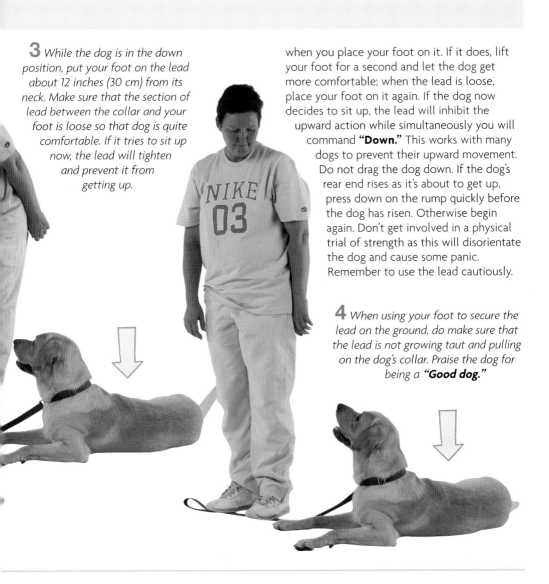

Down Using A Hook

As with the sit position, attaching a lead to the dog's collar is sometimes helpful with powerful or boisterous dogs—this can be then dropped over the hook to prevent the dog from moving away from you. Face the dog and use food or a toy to persuade it to adopt the down position.

Sometimes I pretend to scrape the carpet and this can also help the dog to go down on command. Don't forget to praise the dog when it finally lies down.

Down Using a Push (puppy safe)

This is especially good for less-dominant types of dog. Place the dog on your left side attached to the lead and collar. Stand still and command **"Sit"** at your left side. Once sitting, you may press on the dog's back behind its shoulder blades saying **"Down."** As you do so, you can gently pull the lead in a downward motion to

1 *A hook is a valuable training aid when you need to restrain an over-exuberant dog and keep it under control.*

2 *Use the tidbit lure to get the dog to sink to the floor while giving the **"Down"** command.*

3 *Praise your dog as it lies quietly in the down position. Any unwanted movement toward you will be checked by the lead looped over the hook.*

the floor—the two guiding actions encourage the dog to lie down and you dutifully praise it when it's down. Some dogs react against this push and pull method but not many. If your dog reacts by struggling, choose another training style. Remember to be firm yet gentle; you are not using brute force to guide the dog downward. If you yank the lead down and push roughly on the dog's back, you may just induce a sense of panic.

1 *Begin with the dog on the lead and sitting by your side.*

2 *Command "Down" and simultaneously push the dog between its shoulder blades while drawing it down with the lead.*

3 *When the dog assumes the down position correctly, stroke and praise it for getting the down right.*

Down/Stay

The technique explained in the sit/stay (see pages 128–129) is also used to teach the down/stay. You work incrementally, building up the time that you command a dog to stay in the down position and the distance you walk to separate yourself from the dog. As the down is a comfortable position for a dog, you may build up to longer duration stays, eventually reaching three minutes.

Location Dog Training

Training dogs can be frustrating at times because we often assume that dogs think like us or at least reason the world out as we do. Well, they don't. Nothing demonstrates better

how dogs actually learn than location training. By this I mean teaching the dog to execute all its learned training in any location you choose. This involves two unpredictable factors: the different location and all the distractions that may be present. Dogs that will happily obey your commands willingly in the house often don't appear to understand the basic **"Sit"** command when in another location.

Once trained to a basic level, dogs really need to practice all the exercises in as many different places as one can find. The more distractions they can overcome or become

habituated to, the more steady the training becomes. Of course in the outside world, masses of distractions tend to crop up, perhaps in the form of other canines, cats racing along sidewalks and across the road, traffic noises, or people passing by. The outside world is full of fascinating scents that excite the dog's most powerful sense. It's a recipe that can cause havoc with concentration.

Even if you are only training your dog to a fairly basic level

Left: *Distractions abound in the outside world. This is where a dog's training will really be put to the test.*

of obedience, it still has to learn to be obedient in parks, shopping malls, and other public places. Your dog needs to learn to obey your commands while other dogs are about. In the urban jungle of busy shopping streets, a dog cannot be allowed to cut across pedestrians or pull away to sniff at any other dog it may see. Once a dog obeys all your

commands reliably, then the motivational inducements, such as food, a toy, or touch, are removed. You merely make a command, e.g., **"Sit,"** and the dog is verbally praised when it obeys. That's it. Occasionally the odd toy or tidbit can be produced as a reinforcer; however, all trained dogs should obey your commands with your verbal praise as their sole reward.

It is now time to transfer the majority of your training lessons to the outside world and to practice in many of the locations in which your dog needs to be obedient. For my example I'll use the local park, but your area for training may be different. From a safety point of view, especially with dogs that may run off when released, it is best to get well into the park—at least 200 yards from the entrance—so that if anything goes wrong your dog is well away from any road traffic.

Left: Do remember that dog training is not an end in itself— it has a practical purpose. You want your dog to obey you at all times and in all locations. So make sure that you practice in the park where lots of distractions are around.

147

Training In Action: The Walk To The Park

Dogs often become excited, even overexcited, as we make preparations for the walk from the house to the park. It is normal fun for the dog. If that excitement interrupts you trying to leave the house in an orderly fashion, it is defeating the exercise for all concerned. We need routine and order, and step by step the dog must learn this. I will now describe a few practical scenarios to help you put your dog's training to good use.

We first connect the lead to the dog in the house. If your dog accepts this with general enthusiasm, that's fine. If it becomes so over-excited that even connecting the lead becomes a trial, then confuse the animal by making three or four false starts. Sit down after each one, and eventually the dog will calm down as it will no longer know when you really mean to walk. Once you're ready to exit the house, remember that the dog must not be allowed to barge ahead of you through the front door. You should have already been training the dog to wait at doors while you walk through first as you practice in your home in the first week. The dog should now be waiting for you to take the lead. Exit the house and shut the door in the dog's face even if it tries to take the lead just once (see Leadership Program on page 23).

If you have a front gate, repeat the whole process here too—you go first, the dog waits. Remember that the dog is learning to link each action and command with a reward. Don't forget to praise it each and every time it does what you want.

Off you both go down the street. Now the distractions appear and that heelwork training involving left turns, right turns, and about turns comes into play if the dog begins to surge ahead. Don't let it stop for sniffs or to say hello to another dog, just keep walking briskly. At first with some dogs this will seem like very

Left: Don't let your dog get overexcited and out of control when you put on your coat to leave the house. Make a series of false starts to confuse its expectations and leave "for real" only when it is calm.

1 *Remember your leadership skills: the pack leader always goes through the front door first. If your dog tries to push ahead of you, pull the door shut in its face.*

2 *That is more like it. You demonstrate to the dog that it's your right to go through the door first. Then instruct the dog to* **"Come"** *when you are ready for it to follow you.*

hard work. In that case there is no harm in simply walking a few hundred yards and then going back to the house again if you are tired or feel the dog is getting the upper hand. It's no use losing your leadership edge. However, for most dogs one can continue to the park.

Right: Your heelwork training comes into play during the walk from your home to the park. Try to keep the dog focused on your commands.

The Walk To the Park

This experience is teaching the dog that no matter how eager it is to go for a walk, you have the right to change direction whenever you wish and you will do so if it begins to pull. First command **"Heel."** If the dog responds, praise it, if not, don't forget to snap the lead as the dog tries to pull you into a hedge for a sniff. Executing an about turn does wonders for a dog's concentration as you pivot on your left foot, swinging around with your right knee and walking off in the opposite direction. Off you go, again encouraging the dog to stay by your left side and praising it when it does so.

Practicing the sit and maybe the down will help to steady the dog. Leading it to expect that you may say **"Sit"** every few hundred yards

teaches it to pay more attention to you for that piece of ham when it's near your left side or when it turns about on cue with you. The less the dog predicts your behavior, the more it has to listen to you.

3 *Vary your turns as you go, and perhaps even throw in some about turns so that the dog has to remain focused on you.*

2 *While the dog is walking calmly to heel, praise it and command* **"Heel"** *as you execute a turn.*

At the Park: Find Your Training Area

When you reach the park it's time to practice all the lessons you have been teaching your dog in this new arena, ideally with as few distractions as possible. Practice the following exercises:
• The sit
• The stand
• The down
• The heel
• The sit/stay on the lead or off the lead
• The stand/stay on or off the lead
• The down/stay on or off the lead
• The recall
• Finish with a controlled play period

7 By introducing unpredictable turns and sits, and rewarding obedience with praise, you remain the focus of attention.

6 Use your knee to nudge the dog into a left turn if it loses concentration and wanders across your path.

4 Every now and then tell the dog *"Sit."* It will be more on its toes if it doesn't know quite what to expect during the walk.

5 Give some quiet words of praise when the dog watches you attentively.

1 Once you are outside the front door, get your dog nicely positioned on your left-hand side and then *"Heel"* off down the street toward the park.

The Sit/Stay—Signal And Time

The next stage is to teach the dog to remain obedient to the **"Stay"** command in the park while walking away to the full length of the lead and incorporating hand signals. Make your dog sit on your left-hand side. As you leave the dog, hold the flat of your hand a short distance in front of the dog's face and command **"Stay"** simultaneously. Now walk away from the dog, keeping your eye on it for the entire time. Turn and face the dog when you are about one to two yards away.

Wait about five seconds. If the dog does not move, return to it either by walking around the dog counterclockwise or by retracing the route by which you left the dog. Varying the return helps cement the stay. Once the exercise is complete, give the dog lots of praise. Use food rewards only if they don't overexcite the dog. Some dogs concentrate too much on the food and not enough on what's being said. I tend to use food sparingly—if at all—for the stays.

1 *Give a verbal **"Stay"** command, and back it up by holding the flat of your hand in front of the dog's face. Step away from the sitting dog, allowing the lead to feed out behind you.*

2 *When you reach the full extent of the lead, turn to face the dog, repeat the **"Stay"** command, and back up the verbal order with the appropriate hand signal.*

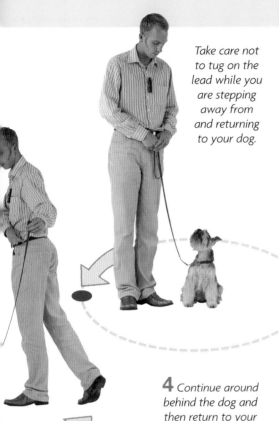

Take care not to tug on the lead while you are stepping away from and returning to your dog.

3 *Keep the dog in the stay position for a few seconds before starting to return in a counter-clockwise direction.*

4 *Continue around behind the dog and then return to your start position with the dog seated on your left. It has remained sitting stock still throughout the exercise and deserves some warm words of praise.*

Common Sit/Stay Problems

The dog keeps following me
Solution: The dog is probably confused— check that your own training actions are correct. Go back to moving just one step away from the dog until its stability improves.

Inevitably there will be times when the sit/stay doesn't go as planned!

The dog moves when I turn and face it
Solution: Make sure you are not tugging the lead. Remember to use the correct hand signal. Try to anticipate the move and firmly recommand the dog to **"Stay"** before it actually moves.

The dog moves upon my return and gets excited
Solution: With excitable dogs, tone down your words of praise upon your return, and wait a few seconds at the dog's side before praising it. Recommanding **"Stay"** as you stand next to your dog helps to stabilize it.

Stay Positions—Time And Distance Training

The technique was introduced on pages 128–129. We are going to extend its use while on location training in an environment where your dog will experience outside distractions. Time is the most crucial part of the stay. If your dog will eventually lie down for a full three minutes while you stand about three yards away from it and will do that consistently, then that dog has achieved a great deal and the training will be rock solid for future use.

What we now do with the stays is to begin to drop the lead as we walk off to stand no farther than about two yards from the dog. We also begin to increase the time we leave the dog in the sit position, for instance, up to about one minute. If the dog attempts to move, command **"Stay"** again. If the dog moves toward you, always go back to the dog and very quickly place it in exactly the same position that it left, not the place where you caught it.

Dogs know where they were placed and can quickly learn to get near you, which is a natural desire. When a dog will stay in sit/stay position for one minute and you are able to return and praise it say three times per lesson without error, then we are making good progress. Don't try to increase time or distance if the dog does not seem to understand the present level of training. This will only lead to you saying **"No"** more often than praising the dog for doing the right thing, and that destroys the dog's confidence and enjoyment of training.

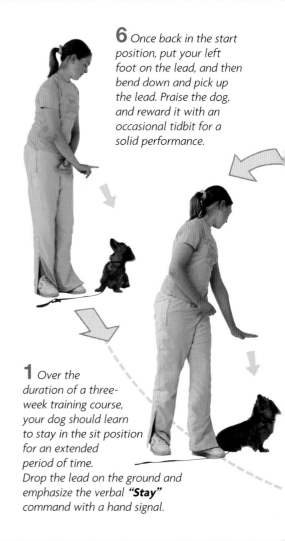

6 *Once back in the start position, put your left foot on the lead, and then bend down and pick up the lead. Praise the dog, and reward it with an occasional tidbit for a solid performance.*

1 *Over the duration of a three-week training course, your dog should learn to stay in the sit position for an extended period of time. Drop the lead on the ground and emphasize the verbal **"Stay"** command with a hand signal.*

5 Repeat the command *"Stay"* as you are about to walk behind your dog and temporarily out of its view.

4 Make the return quite brisk and deliberate. If you dawdle back, you risk the dog becoming impatient and giving in to the temptation of coming to meet you.

3 At the farthest point from the dog, turn to face it and reiterate the *"Stay"* command. You initially want the dog to remain in this position for a minute.

2 As you walk off to a distance of about three yards from your dog, make sure that its attention does not wander. Repeat the *"Stay"* command if necessary, and use a hand signal as a means of visual reinforcement.

155

How Long To Maintain Stay Positions?

1 *When practicing the stay exercises, do remember that a dog will find some positions easier to hold than others. Generally the down/stay is the most comfortable.*

2 *Your dog should now be used to this exercise—you command it to "Stay," drop the lead, walk away some distance, turn and face it, repeat the "Stay," command, and then allow some time to elapse while the dog has to remain obediently in the chosen position.*

During the first week of training, most dogs can be left in the sit/stay and down/stay positions for around 30 seconds or so before you return. The stand/stay may take a week longer as dogs find it easier to move toward you from the stand.

The sit/stay by the end of week two can be extended to two minutes and two yards' distance not holding the lead. The down/stay by the end of week two should be reaching about two minutes duration and may be at a distance of five or more yards. On this training course the stand/stay will not exceed one minute in duration for general reasonableness and comfort. The sit/stay should reach about two minutes maximum and the down/stay about three minutes maximum during week three.

3 *When the required time has elapsed, return to the dog, walk around it, and pick up the lead. If the week two training has gone well, you will be looking to build on it during week three.*

*2 **minutes*** *By the end of week two your dog should remain in a sit/stay for up to two minutes.*

Training Tips

- It is useful to have some hooks positioned at strategic places that you can drop the end of the lead over before you tell the dog to sit/stay, stand/stay, or down/stay. If the dog begins to move or follow you, the lead halts it. If you simultaneously recommend **"Stay,"** the dog will often associate the halting with your command.
- If a dog is moving more than it is staying, which means that it is receiving more correction than praise, I simply switch exercises and do something the dog can achieve well and leave the first exercise until the next training schedule or a little later in the current training period.
- If the dog seems lethargic and uninterested, try distracting it with a quick ball or squeaky toy game for a minute or two and then return to the exercise.
- Once the entire training lesson is complete, always play some sort of game as this teaches the dog to expect that the training will always be associated with an element of fun.

At the end of a training session, play a fun game with your dog or dogs. It helps if they associate training with enjoyment.

Distractions: The Acid Test

By the end of week three the stays should be progressing well. Though you will still be carrying out some training in and about the home throughout the day, the outside training places should be the main focus now. Do bear in mind that if you are doing well, then the down/stay can be prolonged up to about three minutes without the dog moving once.

This is when I start to get friends to walk their dog on a lead about three yards from my dog when it is in a sit/stay or down/stay in the park or yard. Even though my dog may be staying happily at a distance of five yards in the home environment, I initially tend to move away no farther than one yard from the dog when introducing the

dog decoy distraction in the park. If your dog moves, command **"Stay"** in a sharp admonishing voice. Hold the lead for the first few practices. If your dog lunges at the other dog, check the lead sharply and say **"Sit/Stay"**. The idea is that you begin to

Above: When you practise stays in the park, be prepared for your dog to react to the various distractions like other dogs, people walking past, joggers, and so on. You will need to be patient and to use a lead initially so that you retain control at all times.

leave your dog in the sit/stay or down/stay and walk two yards away when it is steady and does not move in reaction to the distraction.

Some dogs stay with no problem whatsoever even when the distractions are introduced. Different distractions affect different dogs in different ways. With some dogs, it's people walking nearby, with others, it's people playing a ball game. Whichever is your dog's weakness, practice the stays while always bearing in mind that you should not place yourself and your dog in a position whereby you might lose control and let the dog get its own way.

necessarily more obedient, although this can appear to be the case. Still carry on with your training on the way home, but do allow for a little more listlessness. This is not disobedience but the natural reaction of a dog who has worked hard.

Going Home

After your training session is complete, do play some fun games with your dog rather than simply letting it wander off to find its own amusement. Many people gleefully tell me that their dogs are much better behaved on the way home after a training session in the park. Of course, they are like children at the end of an exciting day—they are tired. This does not mean that they are

Left: *Finish off your park training with some fun and games so that the dog can let off steam.*
Right: *Remember to maintain good discipline and keep up your training standards on the walk home from the park.*

159

17 • The Recall

Teaching your dog to come to you on command in any location is very important for safety and control. In this section I will show you many ways to achieve this. These techniques work for most dogs. So if you have not yet trained your dog to come to you when called, read on and select the training method you think best suits your dog and personal circumstances.

Why the Problem Can Occur

Why do so many people have a problem with getting their dogs to come back to them, and why do some dogs learn to give their owners the runaround? The following reasons are normally the cause. First the dog may have been punished physically or verbally after it eventually returned by an owner who thinks

that the dog will retrospectively associate his present anger and the punishment with the action of not coming. Well, the dog cannot make this association, and this type of reaction simply destroys the dog's confidence in you. Even if you have to catch the dog, punishing it will simply cause it to associate the action of you grabbing it with an unpleasant experience.

The problem may occur because of a disinterested owner—one who takes a dog out when young and lets it more or less discover its own routines. He or she likes to watch it play with other dogs, which a casual observer might

*Below: A sight to make an owner's heart sink—despite urgent whistling and calls to **"Come,"** the dogs are ignoring the recall and heading for the horizon.*

Below: *If a dog fails to come back when called, part of the problem may lie with the owner. A disinterested handler who lets a dog romp around unchecked in the park may be storing up trouble for himself.*

believe is quite normal. Unfortunately, many dogs will come to regard their supposed leader as merely a pack member, and not one to be listened to. When a dog does not listen, getting its attention for recall training is difficult.

These owners find it hard to attract the dog that has now discovered the fun of chasing other dogs. These owners then devise ways of catching their dog—often asking others to take hold of its collar for them while the dog learns to counter these actions in turn. Stalemate. If you fit this category, I can help to realign you and your dog. When you learn to be a leader, the dog will learn to listen.

This Akita puppy is being left to its own devices as it seeks to socialize with an adult Golden Retriever who is not keen on such advances.

Training From An Early Age

Many dog owners receive ill-informed advice from people who say that dogs should not be trained until they've grown up a little and had their puppyhood and fun. This, of course, wastes the most crucial time of learning. You will appreciate this if you inherit an untrained rescue dog. I train all my puppies from six weeks for all obedience and especially recall. Their natural desire to stay near you helps this training, so don't allow that natural instinct to

Below: This Boxer puppy is only eight weeks old, but in my opinion that is quite old enough for it to be taught obedience training and especially the recall. Puppies have a natural desire to stay close to the pack leader during their formative weeks—this instinct can be turned to our advantage in recall training.

be wasted. As the pup grows, the distance it is prepared to run off from its owner generally increases, its confidence grows, and slowly the owner realizes a problem is developing. Do try to avoid this—train from day 1.

Puppy Recall

If you have a young puppy and wish to get off on the right foot, this is an ideal time to start training. Puppies have a natural instinct to stay by the pack and especially near to the leader(s). The leader is—or should be—you. If you apply some natural dog training psychology allied to an understanding of what the puppy's innate instincts are, then teaching the retrieve should be much easier. Moreover, if you build up a hands-on relationship with your pup, the recall will be easier to teach.

When purchasing toys for your puppy or adult dog, make sure they are manufactured to a high quality. Develop a set of stimulating games and particularly the retrieve. A puppy that loves to retrieve and return the toy to you will learn a powerful lesson. You must control the game, as befits the leader, and you should be able to take the toys away from the dog without dispute. These toys can be used later on to help teach other elements of the training program, but only if the fun and enjoyment of the game has been established at this early development stage.

1 Toys are very useful when teaching a puppy to retrieve and return to you on command. Select a toy that you know your puppy particularly enjoys playing with and call it to **"Come"** to you. Show it the toy in anticipation of the retrieve.

2 Command **"Fetch"** and throw the toy for your puppy to chase and bring back to you. The puppy learns to associate coming to you with a fun game.

3 Command the puppy to **"Come"** when it catches up with the toy and is about to seize it.

4 Praise the pup as it comes back toward you— you want it to enjoy the game and the fact that the pack leader is pleased.

The Dog's Natural Drives

A dog is born with a number of innate drives that help it to survive in the wild like its cousin, the wolf. As a puppy it begins to explore the natural world and the unnatural domestic space that we occupy. It explores all the exotic smells

Below: For puppies, living in our world is a constant process of discovery.

Once a dog has found out how to occupy itself, it tends to form its own little routines. That's fine provided you can interrupt them when necessary. You may wish to call the dog away from a person whom the dog is trying to greet but who does not relish this sort of attention. When you call your dog, its obedience simply depends on whether the motivation to obey you outweighs what the dog is focused on at that moment. That's the crux of the problem. We love watching our

in its environment, it plays with and investigates the other dogs it meets, and it observes everything that is happening nearby. While it is experiencing these natural pleasures, you are often the last thing on your dog's mind, unless you have already begun training and forming a strong bond with the dog in these same places. However much you train, the dog still has ample time to enjoy being a dog at home and the park.

Recall Problems—Causes in Brief
- Owners have allowed their dog to find its pleasures on its own from puppyhood.
- Owners do not take on the alpha (leader) role immediately.
- Owners choose a breed that is too difficult to own and train for their level of experience.
- Owners do not train the puppy daily to come in all situations.
- Owners delay training a puppy and miss out on a crucial learning period.
- Owners do not train recall in all situations, including the home, from the time the puppy arrives in the family.

dogs galloping across the park and running and chasing other dogs. It's a lovely, natural sight. The socialization side of these encounters is also crucial to your dog forming positive attitudes to dogs, people, and its environment. In other words this prepares your dog for life in our world, but it has to obey certain rules to survive in that same world. This is what we call training. Most dogs like

Right: *Dogs' love of retrieve games can be harnessed to help us teach the recall.*

Left: *You must be able to gain the attention of a preoccupied pup to train it effectively.*

retrieving. This willingness to retrieve can be now improved, shaped, and used to help with the recall and other exercises during our training course. I will outline several types of training approaches to alter your dog's behavior. Select which one fits your dog's personality best. Sometimes a combination of one or more methods also quickens the learning process for your dog.

Recall Using Toys (puppy safe)

Assuming your dog loves fetching its toys, we begin by selecting a pair of favorite toys (ideally identical ones) that it likes playing with most. For some dogs this can be an old piece of rope or a favorite squeaky toy that mimics the sound of prey. Oddly enough, to help speed up training we then lock all the toys away in a box except these two. Why? When we show the dog its toy, it really becomes excited at the sight and thought of the game to come. You may be using the toy to teach the recall, but the dog imagines no such thing. It sees the toy and remembers the fun it had last time you played together. We need to focus the dog's attention on us through the toy and make the link of recall training.

Begin by concealing your squeaky toy about your person, then just wander about the house or yard. Use this exercise to break up the others like the sit, stand, and down. Variety helps to keep a dog's attention focused. When your dog has wandered off, call its name sharply, pause, and give the command **"Come"** when it looks around. Show the toy, wave it in the air, and/or

1 *When your dog has wandered away, call its name and give the command **"Come"** when it turns to look at you. Show it the toy as encouragement to return to you.*

squeak it. As your dog begins to run for the reward, praise it verbally. (Always praise a dog while it is on its way to you and not just when it arrives.) As soon as the dog arrives at your feet, throw the toy for a retrieve—don't tell it to sit, just throw the toy. If your dog brings the toy back, take the toy and give the dog plenty of praise.

Right: *There is a wide variety of safe, sturdy, and reliable toys available for dogs that we can use both as playthings and as training aids.*

Right: *Dogs usually love retrieve games during which they can burn off energy. You can use them to break up the stay exercises and to make your training more varied.*

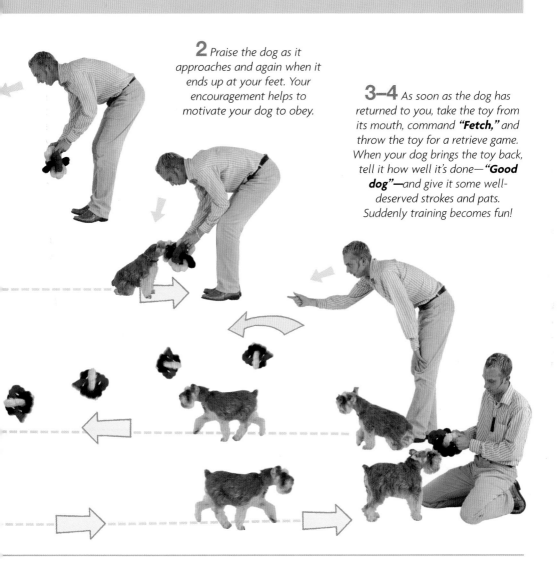

2 *Praise the dog as it approaches and again when it ends up at your feet. Your encouragement helps to motivate your dog to obey.*

3–4 *As soon as the dog has returned to you, take the toy from its mouth, command **"Fetch,"** and throw the toy for a retrieve game. When your dog brings the toy back, tell it how well it's done—**"Good dog"**—and give it some well-deserved strokes and pats. Suddenly training becomes fun!*

Using A Second Toy

Some dogs may not return with the toy. This is quite common, because they instinctively love possession. In this case bring out the second toy and use that one instead. The dog often leaves the first toy for the one you have in your hand. A general dog motto is if you have something, it must be better. Once the dog is coming each time you squeak the toy and command **"Come,"** we may add the **"Sit"** as a new link in the chain. Praise the dog and then say **"Free,"** which is the release command. Most dogs just keep looking at you in expectation as **"Free"** means nothing to them at first. Now ignore the dog and wander around the yard until it walks off to sniff something else. Now repeat the whole recall procedure again using the toy. Practice this between five and ten times daily throughout the first week. If your dog is especially keen to come and is making fast progress, you may also practice on your walks in the park in week one. Depending on your dog's enthusiasm, this training helps to embed the basis for the recall in the park.

1 *Some dogs are reluctant to give up a toy that they have run to fetch. On such occasions, it pays to have a second toy ready that you may use as a substitute.*

2 *Throw the first toy as described on the previous page and encourage the dog to run back to you with enthusiastic cries of* **"Come."** *Bend lower and open your arms if you need to give the dog a visual cue that you want it to approach you.*

Problem Solving

The dog soon loses interest in the toy
Solution:
- Change toys.
- Are you training for too long a period?
- Are you training when the dog has low energy?
- Do you have two toys to use?
- Make sure the dog is getting no toys at other times.

The dog stops coming halfway to you
Solution:
- As the dog slows down as it approaches, jump up and down animatedly and run backwards.
- As the dog approaches you, lower your body and crouch a bit—it will be less intimidating for a lower ranking dog to approach you.
- Attach a short 6-foot (2 m) light line to the dog's collar, so that you can take hold of it as the dog returns. It gives you some physical control and prevents the dog from running off with the toy.

If your dog tends to stop on the way back to you, jump up and down and run backward. This helps to make the recall training fun!

3 *If the dog then refuses to give up the toy, show it the second toy. Normally a dog will prefer something that its owner is holding and will drop the first toy.*

4 *Praise the dog and then repeat the procedure by throwing the second toy for a retrieve game.*

169

Lead And Collar Recall *(puppy safe)*

As we saw in the previous section, the commands **"Sit," "Stay,"** and **"Come"** are used in conjunction with lead control. Lead and collar recall is a basic system of training to come. Place the normal collar on your dog and then attach a 6-foot (2 m) lead to the collar. Tell the dog to sit and stay, walk about one yard away, stop, about turn,

after a few seconds call the dog's name (to get its attention), and then firmly say **"Come"** (the command). Bend down and, when the dog approaches you, offer praise as it comes closer. After many successful practices, you can add the **"Sit"** command so that we have completed the entire recall. Now many of you may have

1 For this method of teaching the recall you need to attach a 6-foot (2 m) lead to your dog's collar. Command it to **"Sit."**

Above: A lead, collar, and tidbit, are useful tools when we teach the recall.

2 Turn away from the dog and walk out to the full length of the lead, taking care to allow a little slack so that it does not pull on the dog's collar and disturb the dog from remaining in the sit position.

achieved this, but find that working off the lead poses problems. At least if your dog can achieve the above, we can reckon that it understands what we want before the next training techniques are used. Of course you should also be teaching the sit, stand, down and stay positions daily, which helps with general obedience.

Practice this lead recall training in the home, in the yard, and in the park. Also once the dog is good at coming to you, add some distractions. For instance, get people to run past you or walk nearby with their dogs. If your dog reacts to the distraction and moves from its position, reinforce your commands in the way described.

3 *Give the **"Come"** command in a firm tone of voice and bend toward the dog a little.*

4 *Praise as it approaches you—verbal encouragement helps to motivate it and keeps you as the focus of attention.*

5 *Reward the dog with plenty of strokes, pats, and attention when it consistently comes on command. These rewards help to cement the recall.*

Recall Combining Sound And Food (puppy safe)

1 *First show your dog one of the food portions that you have prepared. Let it sniff the food but not eat it.*

2 *Run backward, command* **"Come,"** *and then blow the whistle once.*

I find that this method works best if the dog is eating a natural meat-based diet—I do not recommend using dry foods that may contain additives and colorants.

Dogs have good hearing, and most dogs enjoy eating; this method utilizes both these facts. You'll need a dog whistle and some food.

Left: *For this method of recall training you will need to divide half your dog's daily food allowance into ten portions. You will also need a dog whistle.*

You should begin training in a quiet area of the park or preferably in your own yard. Divide half the dog's normal daily food allowance into about ten portions and keep it in a container. For dogs that are very difficult to get back or are not that keen on food rewards, let the dog go hungry for a short while. Do not feed the dog for a whole day. Dogs can manage without food for this period without harm, although this food reduction does not apply to pups under six months of age.

3 *The incentive of a food reward should encourage the dog to run eagerly toward you.*

The next day begin your recall training in your yard. Show your dog a portion of food in your hand, let the dog sniff it, and then run backward, simultaneously and excitedly commanding **"Come"** and blow the whistle once. Your dog should follow the food and come to you. So reward it with a chunk as soon as it reaches you. At this stage the sit is not important—we don't want to interrupt the dog's desire to come to you. Repeat this sequence several times, and then cease the recall lesson—perhaps do some other training exercises. Any food you haven't used can be given to your dog during the next training session. The dog will have begun to link the word **"Come"** with the whistle sound and, upon arrival, a food treat that is not a tidbit but part of its daily diet. This is crucial.

4 *When it arrives, praise it for being a* **"Good dog"** *and immediately let it have the food reward.*

5 *At this stage, there's no need to insist upon the sit. That comes in the next phase described overleaf.*

Recall Combining Sound And Food *(puppy safe)*

Now your dog has a real incentive to come when called for a dog's stomach usually rules its mind. You can use the remainder of its food for lessons two and three. Continue the training for another three days until your dog comes when you command and whistle each time. Keep the dog on the hungry side during the first couple of weeks of training exercises, especially if it is not particularly food focused. If your dog is very food orientated, you may consider training in a quiet area of the park from day one. For most dogs, however, start in the backyard until the dog begins to come reliably and without responding to distractions.

Once the dog responds reliably, drop the verbal commands and use the whistle only, though you may continue to praise it as it runs toward you. Now begin to introduce the sit. Once the dog is coming and sitting happily, attach the lead and practice the heel for about three or four minutes. Then tell the dog to sit, praise it, tell it to go **"Free,"** and walk off. Then repeat the whole recall training with food again. This teaches the dog that being attached to the lead is normal sometimes and that it is released at your will. This especially helps those of you who have dogs that have realized that the lead going on means home. The dog can never know when you are about to go home because you attach and detach the lead many times during the walk.

This training requires perseverance, but it is worthwhile in the end to have a dog that comes when called. In the long run the dog will return to being fed at home through its food bowl, but in that case I take a little bag of ham or cheese chunks out with me and intermittently give the dog a treat for some of the recalls.

Give a sharp blast of the whistle to attract your dog's attention.

1 *As you progress with this recall method, you can dispense with the verbal command to* **"Come."** *Just use the whistle to attract your dog's attention.*

Sound and Food Recall—Recap

- Dog learns that food now arrives at unspecified times during training either at home or outside.
- Dog learns that the new whistle sound corresponds to food rewards.
- Dog no longer eats from a bowl at home during the training program.
- Dog learns that obeying the second command, **"Sit,"** ensures the delivery of more praise.

2 *Now you can introduce the **"Sit"** at the conclusion of the exercise when the dog has returned obediently.*

3 *Reward the dog's obedience with a succulent chunk of its food allowance and a few words of softly spoken praise.*

4 *Finish off the exercise by attaching the lead and practicing some heelwork before letting your dog go free.*

The dog should have learned that obeying the sound of the whistle leads to a food reward.

Practicing The Sound And Food Recall

After you have been training for three weeks and as the dog progresses with the recall, you should use food rewards intermittently to reinforce the recall. You may give a food reward in association with the recall training only once or twice a week. This means that the dog never knows if the food is going to be given but the chance that it may be proffered occasionally

maintains the recall. Of course you will now have a food surplus that can be given to the dog either on the last recall or when you get home. You should continue to praise your dog verbally whenever it comes obediently, whether it is with or without the lure of a tidbit. This takes perseverance, but it is worthwhile in the end.

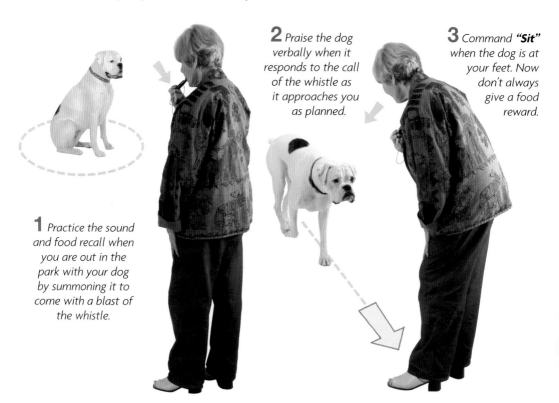

2 *Praise the dog verbally when it responds to the call of the whistle as it approaches you as planned.*

3 *Command **"Sit"** when the dog is at your feet. Now don't always give a food reward.*

1 *Practice the sound and food recall when you are out in the park with your dog by summoning it to come with a blast of the whistle.*

Training Tips
- Don't call your dog just to put its lead on when it is time to go home.
- Call your dog at least ten times per walk to embed the recall.
- Once the dog comes to you reliably, add the **"Sit"** command.
- Play a game of some sort with your dog during each walk to maintain its interest.
- If your dog is still reluctant to come when called, miss out another day of its food rations and then try food recall again.

4 *The dog receives a morsel of food only every now and then, but the possibility of a tidbit keeps it attentive.*

Keeping Within Range
The sound and food recall exercise is particularly useful for people who have mobility problems. The fact that you can attract a dog's attention from a relatively long distance, and have food in your hand that is a powerful incentive to come, makes this a particularly useful and effective exercise. The reward of a food tidbit is a powerful reason for obeying a recall command. The dog no longer expects its food to be delivered only through a food bowl.

Long-Line Recall

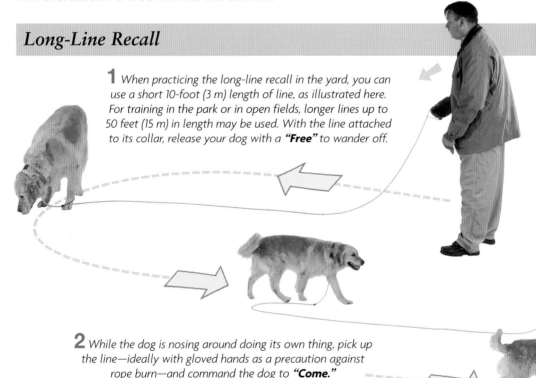

1 When practicing the long-line recall in the yard, you can use a short 10-foot (3 m) length of line, as illustrated here. For training in the park or in open fields, longer lines up to 50 feet (15 m) in length may be used. With the line attached to its collar, release your dog with a **"Free"** to wander off.

2 While the dog is nosing around doing its own thing, pick up the line—ideally with gloved hands as a precaution against rope burn—and command the dog to **"Come."**

Note: This method is intended for adult dogs or very large breed puppies only.

For this method you will need two lines of different lengths, a pair of thick gloves, and food treats if they are being used. (These treats are not the dog's main diet as was the case in sound and food reward.) The skill needed to master the line takes a week or so to acquire. You will need a 33–50 foot (10–15 m) piece of line, for instance an unbreakable nylon cord. A dog hook is attached to one end of the line

and a loop like that on the lead is made at the other end. I tend to wrap the line around a thick stick to prevent it from getting tangled. When using the long line in the park, avoid trees, bushes, park benches, or other objects that the line may get looped around. Open fields and green spaces are best. I also have a shorter 10-foot (3 m) line at hand for when training in my backyard.

3 *If your dog turns and comes toward you in response to the recall command, praise it in an animated tone of voice and start to gather up the line loosely to keep the line out of the way of its legs.*

Garden Recall

Release your dog in the garden on the line with the command **"Free."** Now ignore the dog until it walks off for a sniff. Put your gloves on and take the line in your hand (the glove stops rope burn if the dog pulls away suddenly). You can pick the line up at any point—not just at its end—and take up the slack without pulling. Call your dog to **"Come."** If it comes, praise it as it approaches and then release it again. If the dog bounces around you, always drop the line completely so as not to get it tangled. Say **"Free"** again. When it pops off, repeat the exercise several more times. If you want, you can give the dog a treat when it comes obediently to help reinforce the idea.

5 *So far the line has been a passive element in the exercise. On the overleaf I show how it may be used actively.*

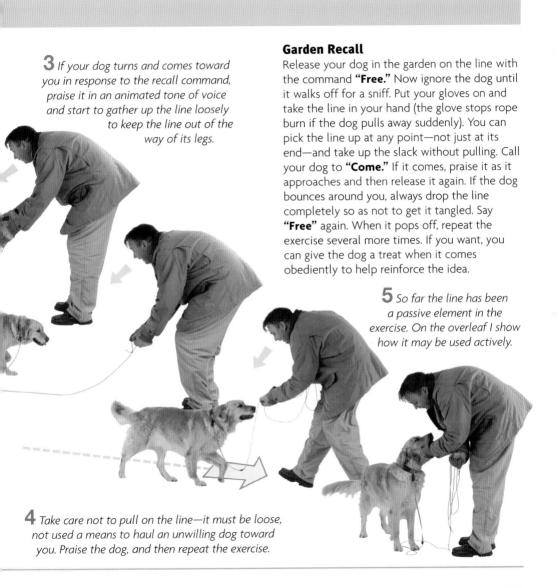

4 *Take care not to pull on the line—it must be loose, not used a means to haul an unwilling dog toward you. Praise the dog, and then repeat the exercise.*

Using A Snap Check

If your dog ignores you during yard recall training, which many do, or continues exploring on its own, repeat the command **"Come"** and simultaneously snap the line sharply, using both your hands if dealing with a large dog. (Puppies or delicate breeds under six months should receive a slight tug only.) Nylon line "gives" so by the time the snap reaches the dog's collar, it is experienced as a mild check. This irritant generally gets the dog at least to look at you. Some dogs become unsure at this action and they begin to listen. (Do not attempt to haul or drag the dog in—that's not dog training.) As the dog takes notice, call **"Come"** again if it has not already started to run toward you. As it comes, praise the dog enthusiastically—for less motivated dogs a little dramatics helps here—jump up and down and run backward as the dog arrives or is heading toward you. This excites the dog, improves its confidence, and keeps its attention. Remember to collect the line as the dog comes in.

When it arrives, a pat and maybe a tidbit will help to reinforce the new ideas. Now take hold of the line about 8 inches (20 cm) from the dog's collar and let the rest of the line fall to the ground. You now can use the line like a normal lead. Tell the dog to **"Sit"** and finish with praise.

Practice this many more times until the dog responds each and every time without having to be checked by the line and comes willingly for the reward and fun of being with you. You will now be in a position to praise your dog for coming, rather than chasing it around the yard in frustration while repeating endless commands.

1 *The long line proves its usefulness when you are dealing with a dog that persistently ignores the command to "Come."*

2 *If the dog does not respond, give a sharp snap on the line to gain its attention once more. Remember—it's just a snap; do not physically drag the dog toward you.*

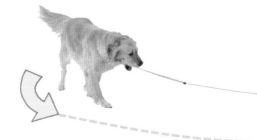

Keep It Lively

If your dog seems dull and listless while training, try to make your performance eye-catching. Wave your arms and run backward—any tactic that will encourage the dog to run toward you is worth trying.

3 The snap check interrupts the dog's meanderings. It should now listen to your **"Come"** command. Start to gather in the line as the dog starts to return to you.

4 Encourage the dog to run all the way back to you with enthusiastic praise.

Long-Line Training In The Park

As soon as your dog will come to you reliably, you are ready to try out this training method in the park using a longer line, which takes a little more time to master. Now it is important to mention here a little bit about the psychology of line use. When a dog is released in the park, it often runs a good distance away from you, and generally more than the 50 feet (15 m) of line. That's fine. Don't hold the line like a flexi lead—it's not a long lead. If the dog constantly finds that it reaches the end of the line and then experiences a stop, it learns the limits of your control and the length of the line. I never want a dog to learn this. If possible try and call the dog back before it reaches the line's end. You can pick up the line at any point,

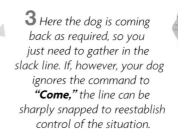

Let the line hang loose—you are not supposed to use it like a conventional lead.

1 *When using a long line in the park, allow your dog to run free at some distance from you, with the line trailing along loosely behind it. Don't keep tight hold of it or the dog will experience a series of checks at inappropriate times.*

3 *Here the dog is coming back as required, so you just need to gather in the slack line. If, however, your dog ignores the command to* **"Come,"** *the line can be sharply snapped to reestablish control of the situation.*

2 *When you want to recall the dog, pick up the line and command* **"Come"** *in the usual manner.*

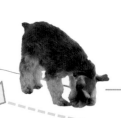

not just the end. Just before the line is about to become taut, tell the dog to **"Come."** If it turns and does so, mission accomplished! Finish the exercise as explained previously. Make the dog sit, wait a few seconds, and then release again. Practice this as many times as possible.

If the dog runs about 100 yards away, the line will be fully out trailing behind it. Casually walk toward the dog and pick the line up. Wrap it around your hand and call the dog again. If it responds—good. If it is slow to respond or carries on doing its own thing, then snap the line sharply to remind it that you are there and it should come.

The fact that the dog can be 2, 20, or 200 yards away from you with the line trailing behind never seems to help the dog to understand how long the line is. It simply remembers that if it does not respond when you call there is an interruption in what it is doing and a great reward when it responds.

Some dogs run halfway toward you and then stop or hesitate. I always run backward repeating the **"Come"** command and praising the dog only when it moves in my direction. This tends to encourage the dog to come to you.

If your dog happens to snag the line on anything, simply clip its normal lead on to its collar for control, and unclip the long line while you sort out the snag.

4 *When the dog reaches you, make it sit at your feet for a few seconds, then release it and repeat the exercise. Aim to do this several times in any park training session; successful repetition helps to cement the recall.*

5 *Finish off the training session with praise and perhaps a tidbit. You might also play a game or get your dog to retrieve a toy. A bit of fun keeps the dog alert and motivated.*

When To Get Rid Of The Line

Though many dogs learn to come quite quickly on the line, I tend to maintain its use for a period longer than 21 days and test the dog in as many locations as possible to help cement the training. Sometimes I will use a squeaky toy, ball, or other inducement to help speed the dog's wish to come to me on command.

The next question is when to stop using the line and how to go about discontinuing it. If you simply take the line off, many dogs revert to being disobedient, realizing that the drag has suddenly disappeared. Once you no longer need to check the dog down the line—in other words when it comes on command all the time—then begin to cut off one-quarter of the line's length each week. Finish by leaving just 3 feet (1 m) of line on the dog for a few more weeks just so the dog thinks it's still there. It just serves as a little psychological reminder for the dog. The line weight should not disappear in one day.

1 *Flexi leads are useful for teaching a puppy the recall. Here a whistle is used initially to attract the puppy's attention in readiness for the* **"Come"** *command.*

2 *As the puppy approaches, the flexi lead rewinds automatically onto the spring-mounted spool that is concealed inside its plastic handle.*

Left: *Act gradually when you want to discontinue use of the long line. Cut down its length each week and leave the final yard for a few weeks more so the dog does not experience its absence all of a sudden.*

Long-Line Recall—Recap

- Your dog learns that when it ignores you, a check will be sensed down the line.
- When it runs to you, act pleased and interested.
- When the dog arrives, lavish more praise, then command **"Sit,"** more praise, and maybe run backward.
- A treat may also be a pleasant reward for coming.

Using Flexi Leads (puppy safe)

A flexi (flexible) lead is a long line and hook that rewinds automatically into a plastic reel with a handle that you hold. These can be used like a lead for teaching the recall exercise over varying distances. However, they cannot be used instead of the long line for teaching recall as the dog would have to drag the large plastic handle unit behind it, which is impractical and defeats the psychology of line training.

Flexible leads are often used for young puppies and for food recall training, where they are helpful for gaining initial control, especially in a yard or restricted area. The sequence of pictures on these pages illustrates the use of a flexi lead and whistle to teach a puppy the basics of recall.

3 *When the puppy reaches you in response to the whistle signal, issue a **"Sit"** command and encourage it to sit still at your feet.*

4–5 *Once the puppy has obeyed the **"Sit"** command, you can give it a little food tidbit and some praise.*

Whistle Recall (puppy safe)

Using a whistle can really help when training a dog to come. Of course the dog generally knows what **"Come"** means but doesn't necessarily realize that it should respond immediately rather than coming when it suits itself. By using the whistle it receives a clear signal over a far greater distance and will come to recognize a consistent sound. You can use the whistle with many different training methods. It can be combined with food, toys, praise, or even a game of hide and seek.

Begin in the house or yard. Make sure your dog has not eaten that

1 *The beauty of using a whistle is that the sound will carry clearly over a greater distance than a voice command is likely to do.*

Left: A piercing dog whistle and a tidbit of food make a potent combination when teaching recall.

Sleepers Awake!
While in the house, if a dog is lying in the front room or near the front door asleep, I will blow the whistle so the dog can hear the sound even though it is out of my sight. When it arrives, you truly know that the dog has learned the sound and food reward. Again this will be useful when the dog is out of sight in the home or park.

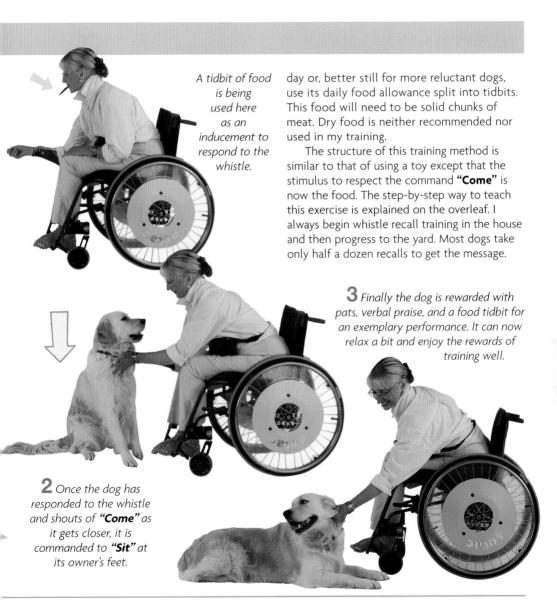

A tidbit of food is being used here as an inducement to respond to the whistle.

day or, better still for more reluctant dogs, use its daily food allowance split into tidbits. This food will need to be solid chunks of meat. Dry food is neither recommended nor used in my training.

The structure of this training method is similar to that of using a toy except that the stimulus to respect the command **"Come"** is now the food. The step-by-step way to teach this exercise is explained on the overleaf. I always begin whistle recall training in the house and then progress to the yard. Most dogs take only half a dozen recalls to get the message.

3 *Finally the dog is rewarded with pats, verbal praise, and a food tidbit for an exemplary performance. It can now relax a bit and enjoy the rewards of training well.*

2 *Once the dog has responded to the whistle and shouts of **"Come"** as it gets closer, it is commanded to **"Sit"** at its owner's feet.*

Whistle Recall (puppy safe)

When the dog is paying little attention and is a short distance from you, call its name, command **"Come,"** and blow the whistle once. If the dog makes little connection, approach it with the food treat near its nose and let it follow the food toward you as you walk back-

The piercing sound of a dog whistle should gain the attention of even a preoccupied dog.

1 *Whistle recall training combines the sound of a whistle, the command* **"Come,"** *and a food reward that is used to encourage a dog to obey its trainer.*

ward a few feet. The critical point is that the dog should be induced to follow you. As it does so, repeat the command **"Come"** and blow the whistle again, but on this occasion omit its name. Immediately give the food reward. Ignore the dog again until it walks off. Most dogs actually respond quite quickly, though puppies often need to use their noses to follow the food in your hand due to their undeveloped sense of coordination.

Once the dog gets the idea that the sound of the whistle brings a food reward upon arrival at your feet, you can drop the verbal command **"Come"** and just use the whistle followed by a treat on arrival. The training will now speed up. If your dog responds very well,

2 *While the dog is sniffing around oblivious to you, call its name, command* **"Come,"** *and blow the whistle clearly. If the dog fails to respond, get closer to it with the food treat and tempt it to follow you as you walk backward.*

sometimes it is difficult to get the dog to leave you alone. This actually means that we have to play ignore for longer to be able to use the whistle time and time again.

3 *By running backward with your body in a welcoming crouched position and the tidbit held out enticingly as a treat, you should be able to make the dog follow you. You can blow the whistle again to reinforce the desired signal.*

4 *Make sure that you give the tidbit as a reward as soon as the dog is sitting obediently at your feet. Then ignore the dog until it wanders off on its own business. Now repeat the whole process.*

5 *Eventually the dog should respond to the whistle alone. You now have a useful new tool in your training "kit" and one that will stand you in good stead when you need to get your dog back urgently and it has run out of your sight.*

*When the dog responds well to the whistle, you should be able to drop the **"Come"** command.*

189

Hide-And-Seek Recall

This training method takes advantage of the fact that dogs are pack animals that find it natural to move, hunt, and roam together. The relationship you have with your dog needs to be close in order to take advantage of these natural tendencies. If you decide to use this method, you need to have already built a relationship with the dog where you are deferred to as the leader (see also the chapter on the Leadership Program on pages 20–27).

Pick a safe place where there are few roads so that if your dog does lose you momentarily, it cannot come to harm. When your dog is about 50 yards away from you, hide behind a tree or bush. Most dogs will want to keep in you in sight even if they do not reliably obey your commands until taught otherwise. While hiding, call the dog's name and command **"Come."** You may also use a whistle to attract its attention if it has been habituated to whistles during training. After a short time the dog will notice your disappearance. If your dog comes running to seek you out, it will begin to panic a little when you do not appear. Allow this to take place, then reveal yourself. As your dog runs up to you repeat the command **"Come"** and indulge in a bit of dramatic praise, running and jumping as if this is the most exciting event in your life. Maybe throw a toy for the dog also.

Below: The hide-and-seek recall is an effective method to use with dogs that like to wander off from you while you are out walking. Although your dog may seem to be unconcerned about your whereabouts, it does like to be reassured that the pack leader is in the vicinity.

Now repeat this many times as you walk each day. The dogs with which this method works become harder and harder to hide from. My dog that is well trained still loves this game of hide-and-seek and it keeps him on his toes while we are out exercising in parks or open countryside. Thereafter you can use the command **"Come"** and the dog will be determined to arrive immediately before you can perform the disappearing trick. Sometimes a tidbit helps to reinforce the message.

While the dog is hunting left and right in an attempt to find you, pop out into view again and whistle for it to ***"Come."***

Above: *By hiding from your dog, and calling or whistling it to* ***"Come"*** *while you are hidden, you arouse a slight sense of anxiety. It will be eager to run up to you when you do reappear.*

191

Spray Collar Recall

Remote spray collars are the latest device to help people control their dog's behavior at a distance. They contain an innocuous spray, like citronella or mustard scent. When the hand device is depressed, a jet of spray is released from the collar beneath the dog's chin forming an aerosol of vapor under the dog's nose. The psychological effect on the dog is similar to, but more marked than, the check administered down the long line. This sends the following message.

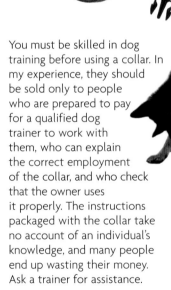

• This is alarming and the dog is happy to run back to the owner who is calling it.
• The dog's determined sniffing or play is interrupted suddenly, allowing it to hear the **"Come"** command once more.

You must be skilled in dog training before using a collar. In my experience, they should be sold only to people who are prepared to pay for a qualified dog trainer to work with them, who can explain the correct employment of the collar, and who check that the owner uses it properly. The instructions packaged with the collar take no account of an individual's knowledge, and many people end up wasting their money. Ask a trainer for assistance.

Left and above: A spray collar consists of a remote hand control operated by the owner and a collar-mounted device that delivers a cloud of pungent vapor under the dog's nose.

1 This dog is resolutely ignoring its owner's commands to come back. By depressing a button on the hand controller, she sends a signal to the spray collar.

2 The jet of strong-smelling vapor emitted by the collar interrupts the dog's meanderings. It will probably look up in a startled way. While the dog is feeling a little alarmed and looking around for its owner, she commands **"Come"** again.

3 The dog comes running back for reassurance. The owner praises it as it approaches and lets it know that it's been a **"Good dog"** for obeying the recall. Do heed this one word of warning—ask for professional advice before using a spray collar for the first time.

Tips To Improve Your Recall

In the previous pages I have outlined several different methods of teaching dogs to obey the recall command. Some dogs may respond particularly well to treats and tidbits; others are motivated by toys; others respond consistently to a whistle. I encourage you to study the different training methods that I suggest and select one that best suits your dog. If one way doesn't work, don't despair. Try another approach. With persistence and application, you will find one that works. To help cement the training, a selection of important dos and don'ts are highlighted in the accompanying panel. On the overleaf I explain how to deal with a couple of problem behaviors that are associated with dogs that disobey the recall command.

Below: *This is the whole point of teaching recall—you want your dog to come reliably to you when called.*

Recall Training: Dos and Don'ts

- Don't chase a dog that does not come on command. This simply makes a game of it and inhibits the training process.
- Don't shout at your dog. This causes the dog to associate recall with your anger—that is not what you want at all.
- Don't catch the dog and then hit it for not coming to you sooner. Dogs don't make that sort of connection.
- Don't train in areas that make your task more difficult with regard to outside distractions. Add these slowly over a period of several weeks.
- Don't train after a walk—dogs lose interest or fail to obey because they are worn out.
- Don't call the dog if you are unable to reinforce the command if you are ignored, even if that means that the dog wanders off where you may not wish it to. That way the dog learns that when you speak, it has no choice but to obey.
- Do make sure you know what you are about to do.
- Do make sure you have all your equipment and that any food tidbits are readily available.
- Do change your location or do some other lead training if the dog appears difficult or confused.
- Do make sure you can train the dog with several different exercises and always finish on one that it can do well.

Useful Reinforcers

- Favorite tidbits—I recommend chicken or ham pieces.
- Favorite toys, balls, etc. Don't give the toys to the dog at any other time except during training. Take all toys home and lock them away.
- The pleasure of playing a game with you.
- The dog's daily dinner given in portions as a reward.

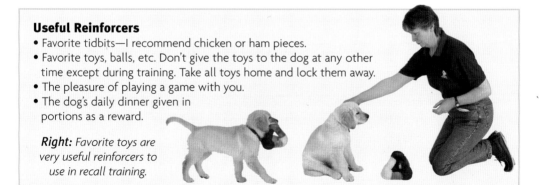

Right: *Favorite toys are very useful reinforcers to use in recall training.*

What To Do If Your Dog Chases People and Animals

The final four pages of this section look at problem behaviors associated with dogs that don't obey the recall command. Chasing animals is one of the strongest natural instincts in dogs. Pursuit and hunting behavior is as natural to a dog as walking is to a human. It is an expression of the desire to chase prey. Dominant as well as fear-driven dogs may exhibit predatory aggressive behavior that involves chasing. They go through the motions but don't usually attack or bite at the end of the chase, although this can change as such dogs get more practiced at it.

The habit normally gets out of control when the dog begins to chase other animals or people persistently. Each successful chase, which is rewarded by the sight of the other animal or jogger trying to escape, encourages the dog to do it again. However, if caught in the early stages, you have a good chance of nipping it in the bud and stopping the habit altogether. This is where successful recall training can pay dividends.

Right: Dogs that persistently chase other people or animals are a menace. Apply recall training to correct this behavior.

Sizing Up the Problem

Identify the problem as early as possible. Excitable dogs like Border Collies and terriers often become chase dogs because their owners ignorantly allow them as puppies to chase rabbits and squirrels in the local park, not realizing that they may be setting the stage for more serious behavior problems later on. Behavior that it practiced over several months becomes an embedded habit.

Some dogs often become bored when out for a walk with their owner. They start to seek stimulation in other animals and people, usually beginning with anything that is moving quickly away from them. With repetition this behavior becomes reinforced and the problem becomes harder to correct. Joggers in the local park are easy targets because they always seem to run off at pace when the dog decides to bark and/or give chase. If the jogger were to turn and give the dog a nasty fright, the dog would soon find pursuit less attractive.

Dogs like chasing things, and probably the most popular toy is a ball. Distraction training works with some dogs, especially those that love retrieving. Teach the dog to retrieve to a competent level. Do not play any retrieve games with your dog except when you are out in the areas where the chase is likely to occur. The aim is to transfer your dog's attention from the chase to the retrieve, so timing is vital. You must focus the dog's attention on the retrieve just as it is starting to think of chasing something, not after the chase has begun. Then, at the correct time, throw the ball and reward your dog with verbal and physical praise when it returns. A spray collar combined with recall training can also be helpful (see page 192).

Unfortunately this rarely happens. The end result is that a large number of dogs develop even worse habits, such as biting and serious aggression toward people.

Corrective Measures

Obedience training is the best corrective method to try first. Consult a qualified trainer and train your dog in the environment where the problem arises. The **"Come"** and the **"Down/Stay"** commands given at a distance are particularly useful with this problem and should be taught thoroughly. With time you should begin to attain some control over the dog. Also check the section on long-line training on pages 178–185. This enables you to gain control over your dog when it is some distance away from you.

Below: A ball thrown for a retrieve can be a useful way of distracting a dog that is intent on giving chase.

Stopping Dogs From Eating Animal Feces

One problem that is associated with dogs that do not respond consistently to the recall is that of coprophagia—eating animal dung while running off the lead. Dogs seem to have a natural desire to eat the excrement of herbivorous animals—cattle, sheep, and horse dung being the favorites. It seems a disgusting habit to us. As far as your dog is concerned this is a dietary supplement to meat and it is only following its instincts. This is especially true of puppies and adolescent dogs who are still learning what to eat—they are very curious and eager to explore a new world.

Prevention Advice

Herbivores' feces is very attractive to many dogs who view it as a supplement to their diet. Wolves have no problem with

digesting copious amounts of elk, deer, and other animal feces, which complements their nutritional needs. They cannot digest vegetation as thoroughly as herbivorous animals can and so eating partly digested matter is a way of getting the nutrition required.

If you are out walking in places where the dog is likely to indulge this habit, then attach a 30-foot (10 m) nylon line to its collar. While the line is attached, don't let your dog play with other dogs as the line will tangle. When your dog attempts to eat feces, jerk sharply on the line and command **"No"** at the same time. This can have an effect if the dog is checked consistently in this fashion. Praise it when it returns to you.

The success of the next method relies on your dog having a favorite ball or toy

Right: A long line—as described on pages 178–181—can be used to snap check a dog that is about to eat feces. Reinforce the action with a sharp **"No."**

that it has learned to fetch on command. Now when your dog is about to go near or eat feces, call its name and command **"Fetch"** as you throw the ball. As the dog returns to you, run backward and praise it when it reaches you. In this way you use play as a means to interrupt the behavior.

Deterrent Methods

Though not always pleasant to the eye, using a cage-type face muzzle is the only sure way of preventing your dog from eating feces and stopping it getting the repetitive reward of doing so, which reinforces the habit. I prefer to use this method as a starter for the first month as it is 100 percent effective in stopping the bad habit. When you come to stop using the muzzle, then some of the other methods can be considered.

The spray collars described on page 192 provide an excellent way of intercepting your dog as it is about to eat any unpleasant matter. The spray is nontoxic and very effective. The spray collar works by filling the air around your dog's nose with a pungent-smelling vapor that soon makes the target feces less attractive. When properly timed, this deterrent method has a startling and positive effect—but you must be taught how to use it properly by a trainer.

Left: A retrieve game can be used to interrupt undesirable behavior.
Right: Dogs that will not respond to corrective training may have to be fitted with muzzles. They are not pretty, but they are effective.

18 • *Keeping It Going*

Once a dog is trained according to this 21-day plan, it should be relatively easy for you to maintain and moreover improve the standard of obedience you have reached. Factors like age, breed, and your own circumstances will ultimately dictate your progress and the end result.

Left: A confident trainer earns the respect of his or her dogs.

Reading the section on location training (pages 146–159) will help you to embed the training in all the places that are part of your lifestyle. If you live in a city, the concentration of dogs, people, and streets encountered there will require a greater need for obedience and good heelwork from your dog while negotiating a busy street. Rural dog owners will need to be more aware of farms and wild animals, and so recall will be very pertinent to them. Heelwork will be less important because of the wide spaces available to the dog.

Combining Training with a Walk

My dogs are well trained because I make an effort and reinforce my dogs' understanding that I lead.

I practice training my own dogs virtually every time I go out to town or for a walk in the local hills. My dogs, Saffie a Cairn Terrier and Gist a German Shepherd, are told to lie down and stay while I open the back of the jeep on the driveway of my house. No mad dash to get in is allowed. They enter the vehicle on my command of **"In."**

When we arrive at the place where we're going to enjoy a country walk, the dogs are told to stay in the back of the jeep while I open the door. That's the **"Sit/Stay"** position. I open the door, wait about ten seconds, and then call the dogs out and to me. That involves the recall and sit in front of me. Again, I tell the dogs to stay and wait a short time, then say **"Free."** Off they go for their five-mile walk off the lead.

That repetition helps cement the training and keeps my dogs listening to me—the leader of the pack.

On the walk I will sometimes call my dogs to me if I see another dog in the distance walking toward me,

Left: Try to practice some training exercises every time you take your dogs out.

especially if it's a small dog. Some small dog owners become anxious when a large German Shepherd Dog runs toward their pet. By calling my dogs to me and then putting them in the heel position, it demonstrates to the other dog walker that my dogs are under control. If all is well, I release my dogs on command and the dogs all say hello and play together. My dogs learn to focus on me when other dogs appear, rather than dashing off because they are attracted by the other dogs. This subtle practice in training reinforces the lessons that an obedience-trained dog must learn. Whatever the circumstances, my dogs are taught that they must always listen and obey.

Even if I meet no other dogs on my walk, I will still call Gist and Saffie to me several times and tell them to sit upon arrival. I pause and tell them they are **"Clever dogs"** and release them once more. Near the end of the walk, about 200 yards before I reach my jeep, I call both my dogs to heel and we walk under control to my vehicle. This is another example of how dogs learn: my dogs now automatically—without a command—come to heel of their own volition when I am about 200 yards from my jeep. I always praise them, and now the routine is well established.

Should I Join a Training Club?

Many dog owners do train their dogs by joining a local dog training club. Unfortunately some end up disappointed by what they are taught and they may become disillusioned and stop attending the club either out of boredom at the way the lessons are staged or because the club just does not have instructors who inspire them.

To avoid this situation, I suggest you visit training clubs before joining so that you can watch what goes on and how it is organized. Among the many thousands of dog training clubs and professional trainers in operation are many that are superb. Take the time to find one that inspires you. Even once you have trained your dog using this book, it makes sense to test your dog's obedience in the company of other dog enthusiasts under expert guidance at such venues.

Right: *A dog that responds well to training is a real pleasure to own.*

19 • Troubleshooting

Unless you are very fortunate, it's almost inevitable that you will hit some problems in the course of the training program. This final section looks at what may be going wrong and gives some tips for getting things back on track.

Perhaps your dog is very good at most of the exercises but is still quite resistant to the recall. Then that exercise needs reviewing. Look at the methods you have been employing, and perhaps select a new one from the options that I give you in this book. I find that the most likely cause of resistance to an exercise is previously embedded bad behavior. Most dogs will train for the recall well. If your dog is struggling, then break down the component part of the exercise at which the dog is failing. Perhaps the reward of food is not acting as a strong enough motivation for your particular dog? If so, stop feeding at home for a while and feed the dog only on daily walks when you are practicing the recall. Even the most difficult dog has to eat. Alternatively use a toy as a motivator instead of food.

If your dog cannot resist distractions—in other words if it refuses to listen to you in training—don't continue to bang your head against a brick wall. This simply teaches your dog that you are ineffective as a leader. Seek out a quieter training area and work there until

Left: There will be days when things don't go quite as well as you had anticipated—don't despair. The situation can be remedied.

the dog is responding consistently well. Then move back to the previous training place. It's a case of being pragmatic.

A Helping Hand

If you have a large dog like a Dalmatian and find that during the early stages of training it tires you out or appears to be getting the upper hand, then ask a friend to share the training with you—split the walk into sections so that the dog has two trainers. Have a break and think about the next exercise while your friend practices some of the training routines. Moreover, a friend can often spot your handling errors if they are apparent, help to boost your confidence, and share in the fun of watching your dog improve.

Make sure your equipment is always at hand. If you are using a long line for the recall and forget the line one day, don't release the dog on that occasion. If you do, it will quickly notice that the line weight is missing and that you cannot check it if it ignores your command to **"Come."** Your previous good work will be undone and at the next training lesson it will be harder for you to assert control. This is confusing for the dog.

Often, other dog owners decide to give you

the benefit of their "wisdom" and will chip in with comments like, "Oh just let him enjoy himself and run around." Smile, ignore them, and continue with your training. That sort of wisdom is not needed. Most dogs can do as they please for almost the entire day, so concentrating on training for a few minutes is no hardship. What's more, the dog will receive its fun and games after your lesson has been completed. Remember, the training is designed to be fun. This means the dog has your undivided attention, it receives lots of praise for obeying your commands, plays ball retrieve games, and suchlike. It is enjoying the privilege of you, the leader, interacting socially with it.

If you have friends who also own dogs and are interested in training with you, then after week one of the program why not arrange to meet and train together? The more dogs the merrier, and the controlled distractions created by the proximity of other dogs will again help to teach your dog to listen to you in such circumstances.

What If I Own Two Dogs?

I find that when most people present problem dogs to me and say that they own two dogs, generally just one of the dogs needs to be improved through training. This can be the case when the second dog is from a rescue center. Such animals often have training and behavioral problems.

If you have one dog that is proving more difficult to train than another, then place it on the training plan in this book and take out only that dog for training. Don't bring the second dog along as a distraction until the untrained dog has been properly trained. It's a common fault that an owner will try to train a dog while simultaneously attempting to handle a second. The vocal commands are picked up by both dogs, even if they are prefixed with individual names. This can cause confusion and prevents effective and consistent training. Once the untrained dog is obeying you and performing to a high standard, begin to introduce the other dog to the walks. Even then, you must insist on the newly trained dog performing its obedience tasks while the well-behaved dog is running free, just to let it know that you command it in all situations. In time, you will have two happy, trained dogs enjoying life in your company.

Above: *Two similar dogs may progress in training at different speeds. Concentrate your efforts on the slower of the two.*

Index

Index

Acknowledgments

There are several people whom I would like to thank for their help in the preparation of this book. A big vote of appreciation to:
Ross McCarthy for his immense help and skills as a trainer and behavior practitioner.
All the clients and friends who allowed us to photograph themselves and their dogs for the training sequences illustrated in this book. Specifically thanks to Spencer Boyle, Christine Brannan, Anne Brierly, Maggie Buckle, Judy Cooper, Margaret Cornwell, Julie Forward, Mike Johnson, Simone Le Boff, Sue McCarthy, Caroline McKernan, Tracey Neal, Diane Peters, Les Read, Tracey Thompkins, Angie Towse, and Chrissie Yggmark.
Monty Sloan, Wolf Park for the picture of a wolf reproduced on page 20.
Mrs. M. J. Litton for setting me on the road to success in the world of dogs.
Judy Cooper for training assistance.
All my dogs.

Colin Tennant, 2005